THE GREAT BOOK OF MICHIGAN

The Crazy History of Michigan with Amazing Random Facts & Trivia

A Trivia Nerds Guide
to the History of the
United States Vol.10

BILL O'NEILL

ISBN: 978-1-64845-011-2

DON'T FORGET YOUR
FREE BOOKS

CONTENTS

CHAPTER SIX
MICHIGAN'S URBAN LEGENDS, UNSOLVED
MYSTERIES, AND OTHER WEIRD FACTS! 128

INTRODUCTION

How much do you know about the state of Michigan?

Sure, you know it's located in the Midwestern U.S., but what else do you *really* know about the state? Do you know why it's called Michigan? Do you know why the state was nicknamed "The Great Lakes State"?

Do you know what historical events have taken place in the state? Do you know which famous pilots were from Michigan? Do you know about the major anatomical experiments that first took place in Michigan?

Do you know which products or inventions have come out of Michigan? Do you know which famous pizza chains started out in the state?

If you have ever wondered any of these things about the Great Lakes State, then you've come to the right place! This isn't just any book about Michigan. Here, you'll find fun and interesting stories about the state.

Whether you live in Michigan or you're planning a trip to the state, you're guaranteed to learn something you don't already know.

Michigan is a state that's rich in both culture and history. We'll bounce around as we take a look at some of the most interesting historical facts about the Great Lakes State. You'll learn more about Michigan's pop culture, inventions, sports, attractions, and so much more!

This book is broken up into six easy to follow chapters that will help you learn all there is to know about Michigan. Once you have finished every chapter, you'll find a Q&A so you can test out your knowledge on what you've just read.

Some of the facts you'll read in this book are surprising. Some of them are sad, while others are shocking. But the one thing all of these facts have in common is that they're *all* interesting.

Once you have finished reading this book, you'll walk away with so much knowledge that you're bound to impress your friends during your next trivia night!

This book will answer the following questions:

How did Michigan get its name?

Why is it known as the "Great Lakes State"?

Which famous musicians were neighbors in Michigan?

What major anatomical experiments took place in the state?

Which famous twins were from the state?

Which NBA legend had a hard time growing up in Michigan?

Which sport originated from the Great Lakes State?

Which city is believed to be cursed by a monster?

What are some of the most haunted spots in Michigan?

And so much more!

CHAPTER ONE

MICHIGAN'S HISTORY AND OTHER FACTS

Michigan is located within the Midwestern and Great Lakes regions of the United States. In 1837, it was admitted into the Union as the 26th state. How much do you know about the state's history? Do you know how Michigan got its name or its state nickname? Do you know which major medical experiments took place in the state? To find out the answers to these and other questions, read on!

How Michigan Got Its Name

Have you ever wondered where Michigan got its name from?

Like many states, the name came from the Native Americans. The name originated from the Ojibwe word *mishigamaa*, which translates to "large water" or "large lake."

Lake Michigan was first named after the Native

American word when European explorers came to the area during the 1670s. The state was later named after the word when it was colonized by the French during the 17th century.

Four Flags Have Flown Over Michigan

Did you know that four flags have flown over Michigan? Well, one part of Michigan, that is.

During the American Revolution, France joined the Americans and so did Spain. Spain laid claim to the land located west of the Mississippi River and had hopes of defeating the British.

In 1781, Spanish raiders went to Fort St. Joseph, a British outpost that's located in today's Niles, Michigan. When the Spanish arrived, they didn't find any British troops there. During the one day the Spanish were there, they gathered loot and took a few British traders as prisoner before they returned to St. Louis, Missouri.

While it's not known to this day what the Spanish raiders' intentions at Fort St. Joseph were, Niles is the only place in the state of Michigan where four flags were ever flown. These flags included those of Spain, France, Britain, and America.

As a result, Niles, MI has the nickname of "Four Flags City."

"Michigan Fever" Drew People to the State

Have you ever wondered how so many people ended up in Michigan? Well, it can be attributed to a movement during the 1800s that became known as "Michigan Fever," which drew thousands of people to settle in the then-territory of Michigan.

When the Erie Canal opened in 1825, a lot of people began to migrate to the then-territory. During that time period, Michigan's population grew more than any other area of America.

Many people chose to leave established settlements for Michigan. At the time, Michigan didn't have basic facilities and also had rough terrain. Families made this decision because parents often had more than seven children—sometimes up to *fifteen* children! With such large families, parents were unable to provide for their children, and they needed to find new lands at affordable prices.

In 1830, the population was approximately 32,000. Ten years later, however, the population reached 212,267.

By 1833, the territory's population was large enough that it was qualified to apply for statehood, which it was officially granted in 1837.

During the 1840s, the discovery of iron and copper was made in the Upper Peninsula, which drew even more settlers.

Why It's Known as the "Great Lakes State"

Have you ever wondered why Michigan is known as the "Great Lakes State"?

Michigan was given its nickname because it's the only state that's bordered by four out of five of the Great Lakes. These include Lake Huron, Lake Erie, Lake Superior, and Lake Michigan. (Lake Ontario is the only one of the Great Lakes that does *not* border Michigan).

No matter where you are standing in the state of Michigan, you will never be further than 85 miles from one of the Great Lakes that border the state!

Michigan is Home to Two Peninsulas

Although Florida is recognized as the "Peninsula State," Michigan is the only state in the United that's made up of not just one but *two* peninsulas. These are the Upper Peninsula and the Lower Peninsula.

Michigan's Lower Peninsula is the southernmost of the two peninsulas. It's often said to resemble a mitten. It's separated from the Upper Peninsula by the Straits of Mackinac, which is a 5-mile channel that connects Lake Huron and Lake Michigan. The two peninsulas are connected by the Mackinac Bridge.

The Upper Peninsula is most often called "the U.P.," but the Lower Peninsula generally isn't referred to as "the L.P."

The Lower Peninsula is much longer than the Upper Peninsula, with the Lower Peninsula spanning 277 miles from North to South and the Upper Peninsula spanning only 125 miles from North to South at its longest point. The Upper Peninsula is wider than the Lower Peninsula, however, with an East to West distance of 320 miles. The Lower Peninsula is only 195 miles wide. Despite its smaller size, however, the Upper Peninsula is still larger than Delaware, Rhode Island, Connecticut, and Massachusetts combined.

Michigan earned the Upper Peninsula in a compromise that ended the Toledo War. Although the state really wanted the Toledo Strip during the compromise, the Upper Peninsula proved to be profitable. The UP's copper has generated ten times the amount of money than the California Gold Rush produced.

Today, the majority of Michigan's residents live in the Lower Peninsula. In fact, only 3% of the state's population call the Upper Peninsula home. Despite its low population, the U.P. does contain 29% of Michigan's total land area.

The Lower Peninsula also dominates Michigan's politics. Maps of the Lower Peninsula without the U.P. are sometimes recognized as "Michigan," which causes a lot of resentment among "Yoopers" (a nickname for people who live in the Upper Peninsula). Yoopers are known to jokingly call people who live in the Lower Peninsula "flat-landers" (due to the area's flatter terrain) or "trolls" (because they live south of the Mackinac Bridge, the same way trolls are known to live under bridges).

Michigan is Home to One of the First Public Universities in U.S. History

Did you know that Michigan is home to one of the first public universities in the United States? Opened in 1817, the University of Michigan first started out in Detroit under the name "Cathelepistemian." The university's name was changed in 1921.

In 1841, the university moved to its current location in Ann Arbor, MI. At the time, Ann Arbor was only home to 2,000 residents, a bank, two churches, and four mills.

During the University of Michigan's first year in Ann Arbor, the university consisted of just two professors and seven students.

The Inner Workings of the Stomach Were Discovered in Michigan

Here's a biology fact for you: the way the digestive system works was discovered on Mackinac Island back in 1822.

During June of that year, a man named Alexis St. Martin was accidentally shot in a store called the American Fur Company.

Although the gunshot was originally believed to be fatal, St. Martin's wound healed in a surprising way. The wound formed a fistula, which bonded to the torso wall in the stomach.

As a result, Dr. William Beaumont, who was a doctor at Fort Mackinac at the time, was able to perform a lot of experiments on human digestion. He was able to access St. Martin's stomach. Dr. Beaumont was able to test how the stomach digested food by putting foods into the stomach and using vials outside of St. Martin's stomach to measure his gastric juices.

Based on his research, Dr. Beaumont concluded that stomach digestion was a chemical process which was aided by gastric juice, temperature, and motion. He also found that the stomach digests different foods in different ways and at different times. Beaumont published his findings in a book called *Experiments and Observations on the Gastric Juice and the Physiology of Digestion*, which was published in 1833.

Beaumont's findings were significant to the world of science. Although doctors were originally skeptical about the studies, they were able to build on Beaumont's research.

Today, Dr. William Beaumont is recognized as the "Father of Gastric Physiology." He was also one of the first doctors to make a significant impact on medical research—and it all started out with that accidental gunshot on Mackinac Island!

This Unique Post Office Can Be Found in Michigan

Did you know that Michigan is home to a one of a kind post office? The state is the only place in the entire *world* that has a floating post office!

The J.W. Westcott II vessel, which is located on the Detroit River, is the only post office that delivers mail to ships. The post office has been operating since 1876 and became an official U.S. post office.

In addition to mail delivery, the J.W. Wescott II provides water taxi service to and from vessels, snack and cigarette delivery, and freight delivery and storage.

Mail sent to vessels must be addressed differently. It should look like this:

Vessel Name
Marine Post Office
Detroit, Michigan 48222

This Famous Pilot Was from Michigan

Did you know that Harriet Quimby was born in Arcadia, Michigan?

Quimby is one of the most important pilots in history. Her accomplishments paved the way for women in flight when she became the first female to ever get her pilot's license in 1911.

In 1912, Quimby also became the first female pilot to ever fly an aircraft across the English Channel. She flew from Dover, England to a beach in Équihen-Plage, Pas-de-Calais. The flight took her about 59 minutes. Unfortunately, Quimby didn't receive a lot of recognition for her achievement, which was overshadowed by the sinking of the RMS *Titanic* the day before.

And So Was This Famous Pilot and Aviator!

Did you know that famous aviator Charles Lindbergh was from Detroit, Michigan? Lindbergh's life impacted the world as we know it in major ways.

In 1927, Lindbergh made a non-stop flight from Rockaway, New York to Paris, France. Lindbergh completed the 3,600 mile flight, which took him 33.5 hours to complete, in a single-engine monoplane called the *Spirit of St. Louis*.

Although Lindbergh's famous flight was not the first successful transatlantic flight, it was the first non-stop transatlantic flight in which a 25-year-old pilot flew solo between two major cities.

Charles Lindbergh, who was a U.S. Army Air Corps Reserve officer, received the Medal of Honor for his accomplishment. His success is what sparked an interest in both airmail and commercial aviation.

In 1932, Lindbergh's 20-month-old son, Charles

Augustus Lindbergh Jr was kidnapped and murdered. American media outlets referred to it as the "Crime of the Century." His death redefined kidnapping laws in America. It's what led U.S. Congress to classify kidnapping as a federal crime once the kidnapper crosses state lines with the victim, which changed the world as we know it.

The Car Capital of the World is Located in Michigan

Did you know that Detroit is recognized as the "Car Capital of the World"?

Although the automobile wasn't actually invented in Detroit, large-scale, assembly-line manufacturing of affordable automobiles *was*.

Henry Ford, who was born near Dearborn, MI, may be the most famous Detroit car maker. But long before Ford made his impact on the automobile industry, another car maker began to produce cars in Detroit. That car maker was Ransom Olds, who started producing vehicles from his Oldsmobile factory in Detroit back in 1901.

In 1908, the Ford Model T made its debut in Detroit. Soon, assembly line-style production started at the Highland Park Ford Plant in Detroit, with the Model T being produced. The production speed was so fast that the Model T became the most popular affordable car to hit the market. At the time, only black paint was able to dry fast enough for the assembly, which meant that a lot of people ended up with the same car in the same exact color. The Model T was produced until 1927.

The Highland Park Ford Plant became a National Historic Landmark in 1978.

Today, Michigan is home to the headquarters of three major automobile manufacturers: General Motors Corp. (Detroit), Chrysler LLC (Auburn Hills, MI), and the Ford Motor Co. (Dearborn, MI).

Although car manufacturing's history is mostly rooted in Detroit, the state of Michigan as a whole has also earned the nickname of "Motor City."

This U.S. President Grew Up in Michigan

Did you know that former U.S. President Gerald R. Ford was raised in Michigan?

While he was born in Nebraska, Ford grew up in Grand Rapids. He attended the University of Michigan, where he played for the football team. While he was growing up in Michigan, Ford was an Eagle Scout, which is the highest Boy Scouts ranking.

Ford later went on to serve on a World War II aircraft carrier. He then served Michigan in Congress for 24 years before becoming the 40th vice president of the U.S., following the resignation of Spiro Agnew. When Richard Nixon resigned from his presidency,

Gerald R. Ford automatically became president. To date, Gerald R. Ford is the only former U.S. Vice President and President to ever serve without being elected to office by the United States Electoral College.

Michigan is Home to This Famous Bridge

One of the most famous bridges in the world can be found in Michigan!

The Mackinac Bridge connects Michigan's upper and lower peninsulas. The 5-mile bridge is the 5th longest suspension bridge in the world and *the* longest in the Western Hemisphere!

The bridge stretches across five miles of the Straits of Mackinac, which is the point where Lake Huron and Lake Michigan meet.

Also known as the "Mighty Mac," construction on the bridge took three years to complete. It was officially opened in 1957.

At the Mackinac's Bridge opening ceremony, beauty queens from every county in the state were transported across the bridge by 83 white convertibles.

These Record-Breaking Twins Were from Michigan

The tallest identical twins in the world were from

Michigan. Michael and James Lanier were from Troy, Michigan.

The twins played basketball at Brother Rice High School when they were growing up in Troy.

When they were first featured in the *Guinness Book of Records*, Michael and James Lanier both stood at 7'3". The twins continued to grow, however, due to a condition called acromegaly, in which the body produces too much growth hormone.

In 2018, Mike Lanier passed away at the age of 48 due to complications from acromegaly and pancreatic cancer. At the time of his death, Mike was 7'7" tall and weighed 360 pounds. In addition to being a part of the tallest twins in the world, Mike Lanier was also the tallest man in Michigan.

The last reported height for James Lanier was 7'6".

This Famous Co-Founder is From Michigan

Did you know that Google co-founder Larry Page is a Michigander?

Larry Page was born in East Lansing, MI. His father earned a Ph.D. in Computer Science when the field was first being established, while his mother was a computer programming instructor.

Larry Page has said that the Michigan home he grew up in was cluttered with computers and science and technology magazines, such as *Popular Science*. His own interest in computers began at the age of six and he began playing with the first-generation personal computers his parents had laying around their house. Page knew by the age of 12 that he would eventually start a computer company.

Page went to Okemos Montessori School (now known as Montessori Radmoor), which is located in Okemos, Michigan. He graduated from East Lansing High School in 1991. He later went on to earn a bachelor's degree in computer engineering from the University of Michigan before earning a master's degree in computer science from Stanford University.

Page went on to co-found Google with Sergey Brin. In 1998, the duo incorporated Google—which, at the time, they spelled "Googol." A "Googol" is the number 1 followed by 100 zeroes. They chose this word for their search engine to represent the amount of data they planned for it to explore.

The pair had indexed one billion URLs by June of 2000, which made Google the most comprehensive search engine at the time.

The company was, and still is, headquartered in Mountain View, California. Its headquarters have been nicknamed the Googleplex.

Additionally, Page invented PageRank, which is Google's search ranking algorithm.

As of 2018, Page's net worth of $51.3 billion made him the 8th richest person in the world!

Today, Page is the CEO of Alphabet, Inc., Google's Parent Company. And to think that it all started out in East Lansing, MI!

RANDOM FACTS

1. Michigan is home to approximately 10 million residents, making it the 10th most populated state in the country.

2. Michigan consists of 96,716 square miles of total area, making it the 11th largest state in the U.S. and the largest state east of the Mississippi River.

3. The capital of Michigan wasn't always in Lansing. In 1847, the capital was moved from Detroit to Lansing due to its centralized location.

4. While Michigan is sometimes called the "Wolverine State," the animal can no longer be found in the state. Back in 2004, a wolverine was found in Huron County, Michigan, but it was the first one to be found in the state in 200 years. The discovery of the wolverine in 2004 was considered such a historical event that it was stuffed and mounted after it died.

5. The longest freshwater coastline in the United States can be found in Michigan. The coastline, which spans across 3,288 miles, is also the 2nd longest coastline in America, surpassed only by Alaska.

6. More than 40% of Michigan is covered in water, which is more than any other U.S. state. There are

approximately 65,000 inland ponds and lakes in the state of Michigan. When in Michigan, you will never be more than six miles away from a water source.

7. Michigan's state fossil is the mastodon. The most complete mastodon skeleton to ever be discovered was found near Owosso, MI. In addition, the longest trail of mastodon footprints to be discovered to date is located near Ann Arbor.

8. The chandeliers that can be found in the Capitol building in Lansing were custom-made by Tiffany's of New York. Each of the 19 chandeliers weighs between 800 and 900 pounds. They are made from iron, pewter, and copper.

9. There are lots of cattle in Michigan. In fact, one of the largest registered Holstein cattle herds in the entire world can be found at Green Meadow Farms in the village of Elsie, MI.

10. Like other states, Michigan has a number of strange (and outdated) laws. It's illegal to get drunk on a train, sell a car on a Sunday, or commit adultery (but those who do may *only* be punished if the wife or husband files a complaint). A woman isn't allowed to cut her hair without permission from her husband. It's also illegal for robbers to file a lawsuit if he or she gets injured in the house when the crime takes

place. It used to be illegal to swear in front of women and children, but that law was repealed back in 2006.

11. The largest cement plant in the world is located in Alpena, Michigan.

12. Sault Ste. Marie was the first European settlement that was located in the Midwest. Established in 1668, the settlement is the 3rd oldest European settlement west of the Appalachians.

13. Michigan was the first place in the entire world to abolish the death penalty in 1846. (The exception was treason, in which case the death penalty was still allowed).

14. Michigan offers 10 cents back for recycling a can, which is the highest amount in the country. The only other state that offers as much money back is Oregon. Michiganders made over $351 million back on recycled cans in 2012.

15. Michigan holds the record for building the largest snowball in the world. The snowball, which was built by ASME Michigan Technical University students, measured 10.04 m in circumference. It was built in March of 2013.

16. Traverse City, Michigan is recognized as "the cherry capital of the world." The city is the largest producer of cherries in the United States.

17. Former Governor of Massachusetts and Republican U.S. Presidential nominee Mitt Romney was born and raised in Bloomfield Hills, Michigan.

18. Michigan is the 3rd largest U.S. apple production state. It's home to 11.3 million apple trees. Apples are the state's most important fruit crop.

19. The Ambassador Bridge is one of the most economically important bridges in the United States. The bridge connects Detroit, Michigan to Windsor in Ontario, Canada. The suspension bridge is the busiest border from the U.S. to Canada in terms of trade volume.

20. Michigan ranks at No. 16 in terms of U.S. chemical production. It generates $2.5 billion per year. Every car produced in the U.S. contains more than $3,500 worth of chemical products.

Test Yourself – Questions

1. The meaning of the word "Michigan" is:

   a. Large land
   b. Rough terrain
   c. Large water or lake

2. When you're in Michigan, you're never how far away from one of the Great Lakes?

   a. 60 miles
   b. 85 miles
   c. 6 miles

3. The Ford Model T was originally produced in which color?

   a. Black
   b. White
   c. Tan

4. Where did the first experiments on how the digestive system works take place?

   a. Lansing
   b. Mackinac Island
   c. Detroit

5. In 1846, Michigan became the first place in the world to abolish _____.

   a. Slavery
   b. Common law marriage
   c. The death penalty

Answers

1. c.
2. b.
3. a.
4. b.
5. c.

CHAPTER TWO

MICHIGAN'S POP CULTURE

What do you know about Michigan's pop culture? Do you know which movies have been filmed in the Great Lakes State? Do you know which famous rapper grew up in Detroit? Do you know which famous celebrity couple is from Michigan? Do you know which influential record label started out in Detroit? To find out the answers to these and other questions about Michigan's pop culture, read on!

This Famous Rapper is From Detroit

Did you know that Eminem, whose real name is Marshall Bruce Mathers III, was raised in Detroit?

Although Marshall Mathers was born in Missouri, he and his mom, Debbie, moved back and forth between Missouri and Michigan while he was growing up. They rarely stayed in any home for longer than one to two years.

That being said, Eminem spent the majority of his adolescence in Detroit and Warren, Michigan. They spent some time living at 19946 Dresden St. The home has since been demolished, but it was featured on the cover of his album *The Marshall Mathers LP 2.*

While Eminem was a child growing up in Detroit, he always had a love for storytelling. He initially aspired to be a comic book artist. His uncle Ronnie Polkinghorn gave him the *Breakin'* soundtrack, which featured the song "Reckless." This helped ignite Eminem's love for rap music. Eminem's uncle Ronnie became his musical mentor until he eventually committed suicide in 1991.

Eminem attended Lincoln High School in Warren, MI.

When he was 14 years old, Eminem started rapping with his friend Mike Ruby. They came up with the nicknames "Manix" and "M&M." M&M later evolved into "Eminem."

Mathers and his rapper friend DeShaun Holton "Proof" would sneak into nearby Osborn High School to take part in freestyle rap battles in the lunchroom. They would also go to open mic contests at the Hip-Hop Shop on West 7 Mile, which was considered an important spot for the Detroit rap scene. Though Eminem struggled to find success as a young white man in a primarily black industry, underground hip hop audiences enjoyed his raps.

Eminem's home life wasn't very stable. He didn't get

along well with his mother, who often kicked him out of the house, even though he worked several jobs to help her pay the bills.

He dropped out when he was 17 years old after doing three years of the ninth grade due to bad grades and truancy.

By 1992, Eminem had formed a rap group called Soul Intent with his childhood friends, including rapper Proof. Their self-titled EP was released in 1995. In 1996, Eminem and Proof joined four other rappers to form a group called The Dirty Dozen. In 2001, they released an album called *Devil's Night*.

After one commercially unsuccessful album attempt under the Web Entertainment Label in 1996, Eminem came up with the more violent alter ego of "Slim Shady." Slim Shady earned Eminem a lot of attention.

The turning point in Eminem's career happened after he was evicted from his home. He, his on again, off again girlfriend Kim and their daughter Hailie were forced to move back into his mother's mobile home. This led Eminem to compete in the 1997 Rap Olympics, in which he placed 2nd place. More importantly, he drew the attention of Interscope Records staff members, who sent a tape of Eminem's performance to CEO Jimmy Iovine and record producer Dr. Dre.

Dr. Dre was more impressed by the demo tape than any other demo tape he'd ever heard in his life. Although he was criticized for wanting to work with a white rapper, Dr. Dre was still confident about his decision.

In February of 1999, *The Slim Shady LP* was released by Interscope Records. The album drew a lot of commercial success and became one of the best-selling albums of the year, though it drew a lot of controversies. It included Eminem's first commercially successful single "My Name Is."

In 2002, Eminem starred in the movie *8 Mile*, which is loosely based on his life and focuses on growing up as a rapper in Detroit. His song "Lose Yourself" from the *8 Mile* movie soundtrack earned him an Academy Award for Best Original Song. Many consider the song to be Eminem's best work to date.

Eminem has made several major achievements. He's the No. 1 bestselling artist of the 2000s in America. He's also one of the world's all-time bestselling artists, with more than 200 million records sold at the global level. Eminem is also the only artist who has ever had nine consecutive albums reach No. 1 on the *Billboard* Hot 100. And to think that it all started out at those underground rap battles in Detroit!

Michael Moore is From Michigan

Did you know that documentary filmmaker Michael Moore is from Detroit?

Michael Moore was born in Flint, Michigan. He attended St. John's Elementary School and St. Paul's Seminary in Saginaw, MI. He later graduated from Davis High School in Davison, MI. While he was attending Davis High School, Moore was a member of the drama club and the debate team.

When he was just 18 years old, Moore was elected to the Davis school board, making him the youngest person to be elected to office in the U.S. at the time.

Moore briefly attended the University of Michigan-Flint, which he left after his freshman year. When he was 22, he founded an alternative weekly magazine called *The Flint Voice*. The magazine's name was later changed to *The Michigan Voice* when it expanded to the entire state. The magazine was funded by money donated by pop star Harry Chapin. The magazine shut down in 1986.

Michael Moore later went on to work as the editor of a liberal political magazine *Mother Jones*. After four months, he was fired after refusing to publish an article that he believed to be inaccurate and "patronizing."

In 1989, Moore wrote, directed, and produced his first documentary. The documentary was called

Roger & Me and was based on Roger B. Smith, former President and CEO of General Motors. The documentary was about what happened to Moore's hometown of Flint after General Motors closed its Michigan factories and opened new factories in Mexico.

Today, Moore is most well-known for his work on *Fahrenheit 9/11*, a 2004 documentary based on George W. Bush's presidency and the media's portrayal of the War on Terror. The documentary earned more than $119 million at the box office, making it the highest-grossing documentary of all-time in America. The documentary received a follow-up in 2018 called *Fahrenheit 11/9*, which focused on the 2016 U.S. Presidential election and Donald Trump's presidency.

Moore's 2007 documentary *Sicko*, which focuses on health care in America, is one of the top 10 highest-grossing documentaries of all-time as well.

His 2002 documentary, *Bowling for Columbine*, earned him an Academy Award for Best Documentary Feature. The documentary is based on the Columbia High School Massacre.

In 2005, Michael Moore was named one of *Time* magazine's world's 100 most influential people.

This Record Label Started Out in the State

Did you know that one of the most successful African American-owned and influential soul record labels of all-time started out in Michigan?

Motown Records, which played an essential role in the racial integration of popular music, started out in Detroit!

In 1959, the label was founded by Berry Gordy Jr., who originally called the label "Tamla Records."

Some of the earliest artists included Mary Wells, Mable John, and Eddie Holland. In 1960, "Shop Around" by the Miracles peaked at No. 2 on the *Billboard* Hot 100. The song became Tamla's first record to sell a million copies.

In 1960, the label was incorporated as Motown Record Corporation, with Motown and Tamla merging as two separate labels. The name was a combination of "motor" and "town," which is a nickname of Detroit, where the label was first headquartered.

By the 1960s, Motown was famous for what was referred to as the Motown Sound, which is a style of soul music that's influenced by pop. Motown became the most successful label of soul music, with its net worth of $61 million.

In 1967, Berry Gordy Jr. bought a mansion in the Boston-Edison Historic District of Detroit. The mansion earned the nickname of the Motown Mansion.

The following year, he also purchased Golden World Records. Its recording studio became "Studio B." "Studio A" was located at the label's Hitsville U.S.A. Motown building, which served as headquarters until 1968. The studio was located at 2648 West Grand Boulevard in Detroit.

Motown had 110 records reach the top 10 on the *Billboard* Hot 100 chart between 1961 and 1971. Some of the most well-known artists who recorded under the label during that time included Diana Ross and the Supremes, Jackson 5, and the Four Tops. Stevie Wonder, the Miracles, Marvin Gaye, and the Marvelments all recorded under the Tamla label.

The company also had a label called Gordy, which Berry Gordy Jr. named after himself. Some of the artists who signed with that label included the Temptations, Martha and the Vandellas, and the Contours. The Velvelettes, the Spinners, Chris Clark, and the Monitors signed with the company's fourth label, V.I.P. The Originals, Jr. Walker & the All Stars, and Gladys Knight & the Pips were some of the artists who signed to Soul, the company's fifth label.

After the Detroit Riots of 1967 and the loss of its songwriting/production team due to pay disputes, Gordy relocated to Los Angeles. The move took place in 1972. The label was eventually sold to PolyGram before later being sold to the Universal Music Group in 1999. By the 2000s, Motown was headquartered in New York City.

That being said, soul music got its real start in pop radio in Detroit. The label's original Hitsville recording studio is now a Motown Historical Museum.

And This Movie/Musical is Based on the Record Label!

Did you know that the musical *Dream Girls*, which originally debuted on Broadway, is loosely based on Motown Records?

The musical is loosely based on the rise of the Motown Sound, Motown Records founder Berry Gordy, Jr., the Supremes, and the Marvelettes. There was even a film, which featured celebrities like Beyoncé, Jennifer Hudson, Jamie Foxx, and Eddie Murphy.

The film is set in Detroit, Michigan, but it was primarily filmed in Los Angeles, California.

This Famous Celebrity Couple Hails from the State

Did you know that celebrity couple Kristen Bell and Dax Shepard are from Michigan?

Kristen Bell is most well-known for her roles in *Bad Moms* and *A Bad Moms Christmas*, *Veronica Mars*, and *The Good Place*. She also voiced Anna in the Disney animated film *Frozen* and was also the voice of *Gossip Girl*. But before all that, Bell's life started out in Detroit suburb, Huntington Woods, which is where she was born and raised.

Bell's first performance was as a banana/tree in *Raggedy Ann and Andy* at a Detroit theater. Before the age of 13, she already had an agent. She began to appear in newspaper advertisements and TV commercials for retailers in the Detroit area.

While Kristen Bell was growing up in Detroit, she took private acting lessons. Her first role in a film was in a local movie called *Polish Wedding*, for which she never received a credit.

Kristen Bell attended Shrine Catholic High in Royal Oak, MI. While she was in high school, Bell was in the drama and music club. She played Dorothy in the school's production of *The Wizard of Oz*. During her senior year, Bell was voted as the "Best Looking Girl" for the yearbook.

After graduation, Bell went to NYU where she majored in musical theater. She left early to play Becky Thatcher in the Broadway production *The Adventures of Tom Sawyer*.

Kristen Bell started dating actor Dax Shepard in 2007. The two met at a birthday dinner for mutual friends and started dating after they met again two weeks later at a baseball game where Shepard reportedly asked Bell for the gum she had in her mouth.

Dax Shepard, who is most well-known for his role as Crosby Braverman in the NBC show *Parenthood*, also happens to be from the Detroit suburbs. Shepard was born in Highland Township and raised in Milford and Walled Lake, all of which are located in Oakland County, Michigan. Shepard graduated from Walled Lake Central High School. He later attended The Groundlings, an improv/sketch comedy troupe in Los Angeles, California.

By 2003, Dax Shepard had risen to popularity in the Candid Camera-style show *Punk'd*, in which he starred alongside Ashton Kutcher.

Shepard went on to star in the comedies like *Without a Paddle*, *Employee of the Month*, and *Baby Mama*.

In 2010—three years after they started dating—Bell and Shepard played alongside one another in the romantic comedy *When in Rome*. And to think that their lives both started out in the Detroit area!

This *Full House* Actor is From Michigan

Did you know that *Full House* actor Dave Coulier is from Michigan?

Coulier was born and raised in St. Clair Shores.

You might have noticed some of Coulier's upbringing when he played Joey in *Full House*. During the show, he frequently wore a Red Wings jersey, which he wore to show how much he loves his home state!

Dave Coulier has also gained a lot of fame as being the subject of Alanis Morrissette's song "You Oughta Know," which she wrote after their famous breakup. So, the next time you wonder who that song was about, the answer is a Michigander!

This Actor Lied About His Michigan Upbringing

Did you know that iconic actor Burt Reynolds once lied about being from Michigan?

The actor first rose to fame when he starred in shows like *Gunsmoke*, *Hawk*, and *Dan August*. His breakthrough role, however, was as Lewis Medlock in the 1972 film *Deliverance*. Reynolds later went on to star in *The Longest Yard*, *Smokey and the Bandit* and its sequel, *Semi-Tough*, *Hooper*, *The Cannon Run*, and *The Best Little Whorehouse in Texas*. He later went back to TV where he starred in the sitcom *Evening Shade*.

Over the course of his career, Burt Reynolds claimed that he was born in Waycross, Georgia. However, it turned out to be a lie. He confessed in 2015 that he had actually been born in Lansing, Michigan. In his autobiography, Reynolds said that his family lived in Lansing until his father was drafted into the U.S. Army. After his father was sent to Europe, the family moved to his mother's hometown of Lake City, Michigan before eventually moving to Florida.

This Legendary Singer is From Detroit

Did you know that singer Diana Ross was born and raised in Detroit, Michigan?

Diana Ross became famous as the lead singer of the Supremes, which was Motown's most successful act during the 1960s. The Supremes are the best charting girl group in American history and one of the all-time best-selling girl groups in the entire world.

Diana Ross was born at the Hutzel Women's Hospital in Detroit. The singer has said that she was actually named "Diane," but due to a clerical error, her name reads as "Diana" on her birth certificate. She was originally listed as "Diane" on early albums and her family and friends still refer to her as "Diane."

Ross and her family lived on Belmont Road in Detroit's North End section. One of her neighbors was Smokey Robinson. Rumor has it that he was also her childhood boyfriend.

When her mother became ill with tuberculosis, Ross's father moved with Diana and her sister Barbara to live with relatives in Alabama. Once Diana's mother recovered, the family moved back to Detroit.

When she was 14, Diana began attending Cass Technical High School in Detroit. Ross had aspirations of becoming a fashion designer. She also took modeling and cosmetology classes. To earn extra cash, she cut her neighbors' hair.

Diana Ross also worked at Hudson's Department Store. It has been said that she was the first black employee who didn't work in the kitchen.

When Ross was 15 years old, she joined a group called the Primettes, which included group founder Florence Ballard, Mary Wilson, and Betty McGlown. After the Primettes won a talent competition, the group was invited to audition for Motown Records. Although the Primettes declined the offer at first, Diana Ross later approached Smokey Robinson. He had the Primettes perform for him and agreed to bring them to Motown in exchange for letting him and the Miracles hire Marv Tarplin as the Primettes' guitarist.

When the Primettes were signed to Motown, one of the conditions was that they had to change their name. Florence Ballard decided on the Supremes without asking the other members, who hated it. Diana Ross was afraid that there would be confusion due to a white male vocal group who were also called the Supremes.

The Supremes set a record with twelve singles that reached the No. 1 spot on the US *Billboard* Hot 100. Some of these songs include "Where Did Our Love Go", "Baby Love", "Stop! In the Name of Love", "You Keep Me Hangin' On", and "Someday We'll Be Together."

When Diana Ross left the Supremes in 1970, she released her own solo album the same year. The album included her No.1 hit "Ain't No Mountain High Enough."

Ross later went on to release a number of hit singles, including "Touch Me in the Morning", "Love Hangover", "Upside Down", and "I'm Coming Out." Her sixth and final pop hit was the duet "Endless Love" with Lionel Richie, which the duo sung at the 54th Academy Awards. The song launched Lionel Richie's career as a solo artist.

Diana Ross and the other Supremes were inducted into the Rock and Roll Hall of Fame in 1988.

In 1993, Diana Ross was named the most successful female musician in history by the *Guinness Book of World Records*. This is due to the total 70 singles Ross has had, including as both a solo artist and a former member of the Supremes.

Ross was nominated for 12 Grammy awards, but she never won. In 2012, however, she was awarded the Grammy Lifetime Achievement Award.

But before her success, it all started out on Belmont Road in Detroit!

This Famous Comedian Was Born in Michigan

Did you know that actor and comedian Ken Jeong was born in Michigan?

Ken, whose full name is Kendrick Kang-Joh Jeong, was born in Detroit. His parents were immigrants from South Korea.

Jeong is a licensed physician. He earned his M.D. at the UNC School of Medicine. While he was completing his internal medicine residency at Ochsner Medical Center in New Orleans, he was working on his stand-up comedy.

Although he's a licensed physician in the state of California, Jeong has given up practicing medicine for acting and stand-up comedy.

Jeong has played a doctor in several notable roles. He played the role of Dr. Kuni in the role of *Knocked Up*. He also played the role of Dr. Ken Park in the show *Dr. Ken*, a show which he was also the creator, writer, and executive producer for.

Ken Jeong is most well-known for his role as Ben Change on the show *Community*. He also rose to fame after starring in *The Hangover* films.

Most recently, Ken Jeong is a panel judge on the

celebrity singing competition show *The Masked Singer*.

His first stand-up comedy special, which is titled *You Complete Me, Ho*, made its debut on Netflix in 2019.

This Famous Blind Musician is From Michigan

Did you know that Stevie Wonder is from Michigan?

Stevie Wonder, who was born as Stevland Hardaway Judkins, was born in Saginaw, MI. Stevie was born six weeks premature, which caused him to develop retinopathy of prematurity. His eyes were never able to develop and his retinas detached, leading to his blindness.

When Stevie was four years old, his mother moved the family to Detroit, Michigan. He began to sing in the choir at Whitestone Baptist Church. He also learned how to play several instruments: the piano, the harmonica, and the drums. He and a childhood friend formed a singing duo. Calling themselves Stevie and John, they played on street corners, as well as at parties and dances.

By the age of 11, Wonder signed with the Tamla label. He continued to perform and record with Motown into the 2000s.

Some of Wonder's biggest hits include "Signed, Sealed, Delivered I'm Yours", "You Are the Sunshine of My Life", and "I Just Called to Say I Love You."

More than 30 of his singles have been U.S. top 10 hits. Wonder has also received 25 Grammy Awards. With 100 million records sold worldwide, he's also one of the top 60 best-selling musicians of all time.

A little-known fact about Stevie Wonder is that his 1980 campaign is what helped make Martin Luther King Jr.'s birthday a holiday in America.

This *Twilight* Actor is From Michigan

Did you know that *Twilight* actor Taylor Lautner is from Michigan?

Most well-known for playing Jacob Black in *The Twilight Saga* film series, which is based on the novels by Stephenie Meyer.

Taylor Lautner was born in Grand Rapids, Michigan and raised in nearby Hudsonville, MI. Lautner has claimed that he was bullied due to his acting.

When he was a child, Lautner took karate classes. He trained with Michael Chaturantabut, the founder of Xtreme Martial Arts. By the age of eight, Lautner had earned a black belt and won a few junior world championships. In 2003, he took part in the ISKA karate event, which was televised on ESPN. It earned him a role on the sports-comedy show *Cheap Seats*, which premiered in 2006.

It was Michael Chaturantabut who suggested that Taylor Lautner get involved in acting. Chaturantabut had played the Blue Ranger in *Power Rangers Lightspeed Rescue* himself.

Taylor Lautner and his family flew from Michigan to Los Angeles for acting auditions when he was called by his talent agency. Sometimes, Lautner returned for school the same day as his auditions. At the time, Lautner was balancing acting, jazz, and hip-hop dance classes, and being on the school football and baseball teams. The family eventually grew tired of traveling back and forth and decided to move to California for a month to test it out. They eventually moved to Santa Clarita, California for good in 2002.

Shortly after, Lautner earned small roles on *The Bernie Mac Show* and *My Wife and Kids.* In 2005, he landed voice roles in the TV series *What's New, Scooby-Doo?* and *Danny Phantom.* The same year, he played in the movie *Cheaper by the Dozen 2* and *The Adventures of Sharkboy and Lavagirl in 3-D.*

Lautner's breakthrough role, of course, came in the form of Jacob Black. It was actually the 2nd film in the series, *The Twilight Saga: New Moon*, that Lautner gained a lot of attention from. Director Chris Weitz wanted to recast Lautner's role due to the physical changes that take place in the character. In an attempt at keeping the role, Taylor Lautner began to weight train extensively and gained 30 pounds of muscle mass. The film came out in 2009, and the following year, Lautner was named 2nd on *Glamour* magazine's

"The 50 Sexiest Men of 2010." *People* listed him as No. 4 on the "Most Amazing Bodies" list. The same year, Lautner was named Hollywood's highest-paid teen actor.

And to think that it all started out in Grand Rapids!

This Movie Was Filmed on Mackinac Island

The Grand Hotel is one of Mackinac Island's most popular tourist attractions, but do you know why? It was once the backdrop of a popular film!

Somewhere in Time, which was released in 1980, starred Christopher Reeve. Reeve played Richard Collier, a Chicago playwright who's able to time travel with self-hypnosis. His time travels take him back to the early 1900s where he finds himself at the Grand Hotel on Mackinac Island.

When he's at the Grand Hotel, Richard meets and falls in love with actress Elise McKenna, who's played by actress Jane Seymour.

The Oscar-nominated movie was filmed on location at the Grand Hotel. You might also recognize the Mission Point Resort, which was the former Mackinac College when the movie was filmed.

The film had to get permission from the City of Mackinac Island to bring cars onto the island. This is because motorized vehicles are generally prohibited from the island, with only a few exceptions (e.g.

emergency vehicles). Transportation on the island is generally limited to bicycles or horse and buggies.

This Legendary Radio Personality Was from Michigan

Did you know that the late Casey Kasem was from Michigan?

Kasem, whose real first name was Kemal, was born in Detroit. He attended Northwestern High School in Detroit, where he covered sports for the student radio. Kasem went on to attend Wayne State University in Detroit, where he did the voice of children on radio programs like *The Lone Ranger*.

When he was 20 years old, Kasem was drafted by the U.S. Army. This didn't stop him from doing what he loved, however. While he was deployed in Korea, he worked as an announcer/DJ on the Armed Forces Radio Korea Network.

Once the war was over, Kasem started his professional career in radio broadcasting in Flint, Michigan. He went on to DJ for several stations: WJBK-AM in Detroit, WBNY in Buffalo, NY, KYA in San Francisco, CA and KEWB in Oakland, California.

It was when Kasem joined KRLA in Los Angeles that he began to rise to fame as a radio personality.

In 1970, Casey Kasem and several others launched *American Top 40*. The three-hour weekly radio program counted down the top 40 songs of the week, which were based on the *Billboard* Hot 100. In addition to the music, Kasem also shared trivia and information about the musicians. There was also a "Long-Distance Dedication," in which people made song dedications. Each week, Kasem would end the *American Top 40* with his famous saying, "Keep your feet on the ground and keep reaching for the stars."

The show originally aired on seven radio stations, but it quickly went nationwide.

The show was so popular that by 1978, it had expanded to four hours.

Due to his vast knowledge of music, Kasem gained the reputation of a music historian, in addition to a radio personality and disc jockey.

In 1988, Casey Kasem ended up leaving *American Top 40* due to a contract dispute. Kasem returned in 1998, however, and continued with the show until 2004.

In addition to being a famous radio personality, Kasem also dabbled in acting and voice acting. He was the voice of "Shaggy" in *Scooby-Doo* for many years. He also provided the voices of characters in *Sesame Street* and the animated version of *Transformers*.

Although Casey Kasem passed away in 2014, his legacy lives on in the form of *American Top 40*, which is currently hosted by Ryan Seacrest.

"The Queen of Soul" Began Her Career Singing at a Church in Detroit

Did you know that Aretha Franklin, the "Queen of Soul," grew up in Michigan?

Although she was born in Memphis, Tennessee, Aretha Franklin's family moved to Detroit by the time she was five years old. Her father was a Pastor at New Bethel Baptist Church in Detroit.

After her mother died of a heart attack when Aretha was just 10 years old, she learned how to play the piano by ear.

Aretha Franklin began to sing at New Bethel Baptist Church. By the age of 12, Aretha began to travel with her father, who delivered his famous sermons at churches across the country. Franklin would sing at the churches they visited.

Aretha's father became her manager and helped her sign her first record deal with J.V.B. Records. Her first album, *Spirituals*, was recorded at New Bethel Baptist Church.

Franklin and her father continued on their travels. In California, she met singer, Sam Cooke.

When Aretha Franklin was 16 years old, she went on tour with Martin Luther King, Jr. She also sang at his funeral in 1968.

When she was 18 years old, Aretha Franklin decided

that she wanted to follow in the footsteps of Sam Cooke and pursue a career in pop music. She and her father moved to New York where they worked on a two-track demo tape.

Franklin's demo drew the attention of several record labels: Columbia Records, Sam Cooke's label RCA, and Berry Gordy's Tamla label. Aretha's father felt that Tamla wasn't established enough yet and he didn't want his daughter to sign with RCA. Aretha, ultimately, signed with Columbia Records.

In 1961, Aretha Franklin's single "Won't Be Long" was released. The song hit No. 76 on the *Billboard* Hot 100 and also reached No. 7 on the R&B chart. Her song "Rock-a-Bye Your Baby with a Dixie Melody" became her first top 40 single, as well as her first international hit.

Franklin went on to sign with Atlanta Records, which is what brought her real commercial success.

During the 1960s, radio personality Pervis Spann dubbed Franklin the "Queen of Soul." The nickname stuck.

Over the course of her career, Franklin recorded 112 singles that hit the *Billboard* charts. Some of her most famous songs include "Respect", "Chain of Fools", "(You Make Me Feel Like) A Natural Woman", and "I Say a Little Prayer."

Franklin won a total of 18 Grammy Awards. She won the first eight awards to ever be given for "Best Female R&B Vocal Performance." With more than 75 million records sold globally, Franklin is one of the best-selling musicians of all-time.

Additionally, Franklin was inducted into the Rock and Roll Hall of Fame, the UK Music Hall of Fame, and the Gospel Music Hall of Fame. *Rolling Stone* magazine also ranked her as No. 1 on their list of the "100 Greatest Singers of All Time" in 2010.

And it all started out at New Bethel Baptist Church in Detroit, Michigan!

The "Queen of Pop" Also Hails from the State

Did you know that the "Queen of Pop" was born in Bay City, Michigan?

Madonna was raised in the Detroit suburbs of what is known today as Rochester Hills. When she was a child, her father got her classical piano lessons, but she stopped them to pursue ballet lessons instead.

Madonna attended Rochester Adams High School. She was a straight-A student and was on the cheerleading squad. Upon graduation, Madonna received a dance scholarship to the University of Michigan.

Madonna dropped out of college and moved to New York City. She worked at Dunkin Donuts while she took classes at the Alvin Ailey American Dance Theater and went on to perform with Pearl Lang Dance Theater.

She went on to work as a backup dancer for musicians. She worked as a backup dancer and singer for Patrick Hernandez in 1979. At the time, she and musician Dan Gilroy became romantically involved. The two formed a rock band called the Breakfast Club. Madonna sang and played the guitar and drums.

A year or so later, Madonna left Breakfast Club. She and Stephen Bray, her boyfriend at the time, formed a band called Emmy. They wrote songs together, but in the end, Madonna decided to go solo. She drew the interest of record producer Mark Kamins, who helped her get a recording deal with Sire Records.

Madonna's first two singles "Everybody" and "Burning Up" became club hits in America. *Billboard* magazine listed "Burning Up" as No. 3 on their Hot Dance Club Songs chart.

Madonna's second studio album, *Like a Virgin*, helped her rise to fame. The album became the first by any female artist to sell more than 5 million copies in the U.S. The album went on to sell more than 21 million copies globally. The single "Like a Virgin" was her first to reach No. 1 on the *Billboard* Hot 100.

Madonna went on to release a number of other hits,

including "La Isla Bonita", "Like a Prayer", "Vogue", "Take a Bow", "Music", and "4 Minutes."

She also dabbled in acting, starring in a number of films, including *Evita*, which earned her a Golden Globe Award for Best Actress.

Madonna has sold more than 300 million records worldwide, which makes her the best-selling female recording artist of all-time, according to *Guinness World Records*.

RANDOM FACTS

1. Sonny Bono, whose birth name was Salvatore Bono, was born in Detroit, Michigan. While he was growing up in Michigan, his mom used to call him "Sono," which eventually evolved into the nickname "Sonny."

2. Kid Rock, whose real name is Robert Ritchie, was born in Romeo, Michigan. He took part in many talent shows in the Detroit area when he was growing up.

3. Actor Tom Selleck was born in Detroit, Michigan. Selleck is known for his roles *Magnum, P.I.*, *Blue Bloods*, and *Three Men and a Baby*.

4. Mike Posner, who's famous for his hit single "Cooler Than Me," was born in Detroit, MI. He was raised in Southfield, Michigan and graduated from Groves High School.

5. Actor and former NFL player Terry Crews is from Michigan. The celebrity was born and raised in Flint, Michigan and attended the Interlochen Center for the Arts. Crews is most well-known for his roles in *White Chicks*, *Everybody Hates Chris*, *Are We There Yet?* and *Brooklyn 99*.

6. Alice Cooper, who is known as the "Godfather of Shock Rock," was born in Detroit.

7. Model/actress Kate Upton was born in St. Joseph, Michigan. Upton appeared in the *Sports Illustrated Swimsuit Issue* in 2011 and was the cover model in 2012, 2013, and 2017. Upton was also on the 100th-anniversary cover of *Vanity Fair*. As an actress, she starred in *Tower Heist*, *The Other Woman*, and *The Layover*.

8. Actress Selma Blair is most well-known for her roles in *Cruel Intentions, Legally Blonde,* and *The Sweetest Thing*. Blair was born in Southfield, the metro area of Detroit, MI. She attended Hillel Day School in Farmington Hills and Cranbrook Kingswood in Bloomfield Hills.

9. Iggy Pop was born in Muskegon, Michigan and raised in a trailer park in Ypsilanti, Michigan. Iggy Pop, who was born James Newell Osterberg Jr., is recognized as the "Godfather of Punk." He was the lead singer of the punk band the Stooges.

10. Actor/stand-up comedian David Spade is from Birmingham, Michigan. He's most well-known for his roles in *Tommy Boy, Joe Dirt, Joe Dirt 2, Grown Ups, Grown Ups 2, Rules of Engagement,* and *8 Simple Rules.* Spade voiced Kuzco in Disney's *The Emperor's New Groove.*

11. Actor Lee Majors was born in Wyandotte, Michigan. Majors is most well-known for playing Heath Barkley in the American Western TV

series *The Big Valley*. He also played as Colonel Steve Austin in *The Six Million Dollar Man* and Colt Seavers in the tv series *The Fall Guy*.

12. Actress Lily Tomlin was born in Detroit. Tomlin attended Cass Technical High School in Midtown Detroit. She was nominated for a Golden Globe award for the Best Lead Actress for her role as Margo Sperling in *The Late Show*. Tomlin has also played in *9 to 5, Tea with Mussolini, I Heart Huckabees,* and *Grandma*. Most recently, she has starred as Frankie in *Grace and Frankie*, alongside Jane Fonda. The role has earned her 4 Emmy nominations.

13. Actor Robert Wagner was born in Detroit, Michigan. He's most noted for his roles in the *Austin Powers* movies and *The Pink Panther*. Wagner has been named as a primary suspect in the ongoing investigation of the 1981 death of his wife Natalie Wood.

14. Christie Brinkley rose to fame when she appeared in the *Sports Illustrated Swimsuit* issues during the late 1970s and early 1980s. Brinkley was also the face of CoverGirl for a whopping 25 years. The model was born in Monroe, Michigan.

15. Academy Award-winning actress Ellen Burstyn was born in Detroit and attended Cass Technical High School in Midtown Detroit. She played in

The Last Picture Show, The Exorcist, and *Alice Doesn't Live Here Anymore,* which she won the Academy Award for. She also played in the 2014 film *Flowers in the Attic,* which is based on the novel by V.C. Andrews of the same title.

16. The late Glenn Frey was born in Detroit and raised in Royal Oak, Michigan. Frey first began playing the guitar when he was five years old. Later on, he switched to playing the guitar and started playing rock music in Detroit. One of his bands was called Subterranean. Glenn Frey later founded and was the frontrunner/lead vocalist of the rock band the Eagles. When the Eagles broke up in 1980, Frey saw success as a solo artist.

17. Actress Megan Boone was born in Petoskey, MI. Boone is most well-known for her role as Elizabeth Keen in the TV series *The Blacklist.* She's also had roles in the show *Law & Order: LA,* and in the films *My Bloody Valentine 3D* and *Step Up Revolution.*

18. Actress Crystal Reed is most well-known for her roles as Allison Argent in the MTV series *Teen Wolf* and Sofia Falcone in the show *Gotham.* The actress was born and raised in Roseville, MI. She attended Roseville High School where she was on the high school dance team. Reed also played in the local community theater's renditions of *Annie, Grease,* and *Fiddler on the Roof.*

19. Smokey Robinson, who was born with the name William Robinson Jr., was born in Detroit. The nickname "Smokey Joe" was given to him by his uncle when he was a child. Robinson attended Northern High School and was neighbors with both Diana Ross and Aretha Franklin on Belmont Road. Smokey Robinson went on to become the frontman of the Motown group the Miracles. When he retired from the group, he started a career as a solo artist. Robinson was inducted into the Rock and Roll Hall of Fame.

20. Although it's often claimed that electronic music was born in Detroit, that's not entirely true. Techno, however, was invented in Detroit. During the 1980s, the Belleville Three were the first to combine electronic styles with futuristic themes. It paved the way for the techno genre, which dominated dance for decades later.

Test Yourself – Questions

1. Which record label was Eminem's *Slim Shady LP* released under?

   a. Slim Shady Productions
   b. Interscope Records
   c. Motown Records

2. Where was *Somewhere in Time* filmed?

   a. Detroit
   b. Grand Rapids
   c. Mackinac Island

3. Which actor lied about growing up in Michigan?

   a. Robert Wagner
   b. Dax Shepard
   c. Burt Reynolds

4. Which musician from Michigan is the best-selling female musician of all time, according to *Guinness World Records*?

   a. Madonna
   b. Diana Ross
   c. Aretha Franklin

5. Which music genre got its start in Michigan?

   a. Electronic
   b. Techno
   c. Trance

Answers

1. b.

2. c.

3. c.

4. a.

5. b.

CHAPTER THREE

MICHIGAN'S INVENTIONS, IDEAS, AND MORE

Have you ever wondered what inventions have come from Michigan? Several well-known products and businesses have originated from the Great Lakes State. Michigan is also home to a number of inventions that are popular among the locals in the state. Did you know which famous pizza chains have come from the state? Do you know which Michigan town is known as the "Cereal Capital of the World"? Read on to learn the answers to these questions and more!

Breakfast Cereal

Did you know that not just one but two of the country's most popular cereal brands got their start in Battle Creek, Michigan? The city is nicknamed the "Cereal Capital of the World."

Back in 1906, W.K. Kellogg opened the Toasted Corn Flake Company in Battle Creek. The company opened after W.K. Kellogg and his brother, John Harvey Kellogg, tried to produce granola. While they failed, they accidentally discovered that they were able to produce wheat berry flakes. This led them to learn how to flake corn. Today, the company is known as Kellogg's!

Post also got its start in Battle Creek, MI. It was founded by C.W. Post back in 1895, who developed a "cereal beverage" that he called Postum. Post had previously been a patient at the Battle Creek Sanitarium, which was run by John Harvey Kellogg. Post was inspired by the food that was served at the company to start his own company.

In 1897, Post developed his first cereal, which he called Grape-Nuts. In 1904, he developed another cereal called Elijah's Manna, which was later renamed Post Toasties.

The Postum Cereals company went on to acquire Jell-O gelatin, Baker's Chocolate, and Maxwell House coffee during the 1920s. The company changed its name to General Foods Corporation in 1929. The company was eventually acquired by Philip Morris Companies in 1985, who merged with Kraft Foods. The company was renamed Kraft General Foods and then later Kraft Foods.

In 2007, Kraft decided to merge Post Cereals with Ralcorp Holdings. The name of that company was

Post Food, LLC. Then in 2011, Ralcorp decided to make Post Foods its own separate company.

By 2015, Post Foods had purchased MOM Brands, which created the 3rd largest breakfast cereal in America. Although the company, which is now known as Post Consumer Brands, is now headquartered in Lakeville, Minnesota, it all started out in Battle Creek, MI!

Although Battle Creek is most famous as being the birthplace of the Kellogg's and Post cereal brands, the city was once home to 80 cereal companies.

Ginger Ale

Although ginger ale actually was first invented in Ireland back in 1851, American ginger ale originated from Michigan! It was also the first soda pop (as it's called by Michiganders) to ever be sold in the United States!

In 1862, a Detroit-based pharmacist named James Vernor had attempted to create a new beverage before he left to serve in the Civil War. When Vernor returned to Detroit four years later, he found that the drink, which he had stored in an oak case, had developed a delightful gingery flavor.

The ginger ale, which was named Vernors Ginger Ale after its inventor, is still available today.

Boston Coolers are a popular beverage in Michigan.

It's the Vernors Ginger Ale version of a root beer float. The ginger ale is mixed with creamy vanilla ice cream. It's a popular treat among Michiganders in the summertime and can commonly be found at walk-up ice cream shops. It was named a "Boston Cooler" after Detroit's Boston Edison district—*not* Boston, Massachusetts.

Gerber's Baby Food

It's hard to imagine a world without baby food, but the invention didn't come around until 1927 when Daniel Frank Gerber founded it. Gerber's father owned the Fremont Canning Company in Fremont, Michigan, which produced canned fruits and vegetables.

His wife, Dorothy, started to make hand-strained food for their 7-month-old daughter Sally at the recommendation of their pediatrician. The task proved to be difficult, however. According to most versions of the story, Dorothy suggested that her husband should start selling baby food to make life easier for mothers. Daniel Frank Gerber saw the business potential in his wife's idea and started to make canned baby food.

The first five baby foods that Gerber released to the market were prunes, carrots, spinach, strained peas, and beef vegetable soup.

By 1928, Gerber's baby food was distributed throughout the entire United States.

Gerber, which was purchased by Nestlé for $5.5 billion in 2007, is the most well-known baby food brand on the market. Today, the company offers more than 190 products and can be found in 80 countries.

Road Lines

Have you ever wondered who you can thank for inventing those yellow and white road lines? The answer is Edward N. Hines, who was a member of the Wayne County Road Commission of Wayne County, Michigan.

You may be wondering where Hines came up with the idea of painting a line down the center of a road to separate traffic in opposite directions. His inspiration actually came from a leaky milk wagon! He had watched the wagon leave a trail of milk down the street, which gave him the idea that you could do the same thing with paint.

In 1911, Hines tested out his idea on River Road in Trenton in Wayne County, Michigan. Within 11 years, all of the major roads in Wayne County had painted center lines.

There's no doubt that Hines' idea is one of the most important traffic safety devices in the history of highway transportation. And it all started out in Michigan!

Synthetic Penicillin

Did you know that a Michigander invented synthetic penicillin?

During World War II, the United States and Great Britain spent a combined $20 million in an attempt at synthesizing penicillin. Their attempt failed.

In fact, most experts thought it couldn't be done. They thought it was impossible. That is, until Battle Creek native John C. Sheehan proved them wrong in 1957.

Sheehan, who was a chemist, earned his Ph.D. at the University of Michigan. He was working at the Massachusetts Institute of Technology (MIT) when he managed to complete the first chemical synthesis of 1957.

In 1948, Sheehan had begun to research penicillin synthesis. He was able to develop new methods for synthesizing peptides.

While Sheehan's initial synthesis wasn't ideal for mass production, one of the compounds of his synthesis was 6-amino penicillanic acid (or 6-APA), which is the nucleus of penicillin. This compound allowed for new forms of penicillin to be created and, ultimately, mass production.

Fiber Optics

Have you ever wondered who to credit for fiber optics?

Well, you can thank Lansing, Michigan native Donald B. Keck. In 1970, Keck, who earned a Ph.D. from Michigan State University, changed the world forever. He helped in the development of the first optical fiber that could be widely used in telecommunications.

Rather than trying to improve existing fibers by using higher-quality raw materials, they experimented with new materials, including pure silica.

During a series of experiments, Keck had measured a batch of fibers that he had heat-treated. He was the first to notice that light passed through the 65-foot fiber without any less.

Using heat-treated titanium-doped silica, Keck and his team were able to design the first low-loss optic fiber.

La-Z-Boy

Did you know that La-Z-Boy Furniture got its start in the Great Lakes State?

It all started out back in 1928 when two cousins named Edward M. Knabusch and Edwin J. Shoemaker decided to go into business together and invest in a furniture store located in Monroe, Michigan.

The cousins decided that they wanted to design a chair for relaxation. Their invention was a reclining wood-slat porch chair, which they later upholstered. They marketed their design as a "year-round chair."

The chair turned out to be a huge success. They held a contest to name their design, with "La-Z-Boy" being the winner.

Today, La-Z-Boy makes recliners, sofas, chairs, sleeper sofas, and more. La-Z-Boy furniture can be found at thousands of retailers throughout the country, as well as internationally. And it all started out in Monroe, MI!

Three-Color Traffic Lights

Did you know that three-color traffic lights originated from Michigan?

The credit goes to William Potts, a police officer, who added a yellow light to the original four-way traffic signal.

The idea came about because Pott was concerned about how police officers at four different light signals weren't able to change their lights at the same time. The answer to the problem? A third light. Amber was chosen because it was the same color used on the railroad. Potts was also responsible for placing a timer with the light to help better control city traffic.

Potts' first traffic light was placed at the corner of Michigan and Woodward avenues in 1920.

Potts never filed a patent for his invention.

Domino's Pizza

Did you know that Domino's Pizza started out in Michigan?

In 1963, brothers Tom and James Monaghan bought DomiNick's, which had been a small pizza restaurant located in Ypsilanti, Michigan. The brothers paid $1,400 for the store. Although Tom and James originally planned it to be a joint venture, James didn't want to quit his full-time post office job to split work hours. James traded his half of the business for the Volkswagen Beetle that the brothers had been using for pizza deliveries.

Within two years, Tom Monaghan had bought two more pizzerias, which were located in the same county. Although Monaghan wanted to call the other pizzerias DomiNick's, the original owner forbade him from using it. One of the pizza delivery drivers suggested "Domino's." Tom Monaghan loved the idea and renamed the original pizzeria Domino's Pizza, Inc.

The Domino's logo originally had three dots. Each

dot represented the first three stores that Monaghan had owned in 1965. Although Monaghan's original plan had been to add a new dot for every pizzeria he opened, Domino's began to grow too rapidly.

The first Domino's franchise opened in 1967. By 1978, there were 200 Domino's stores.

The rest is history. As of 2018, Domino's was the largest pizza chain, in terms of sales, in the world.

Domino's Pizza is currently headquartered in Ann Arbor, Michigan.

Radio News

Did you know that radio news started out in Michigan?

The first radio station to ever broadcast a news program was Detroit's station 8MK, which was later renamed WWJ.

The first radio news program was broadcasted in August of 1920.

WWJ also claims to be the oldest radio station in the United States. However, KDKA in Pittsburgh has been disputing that claim for nearly 100 years.

Meijer

Did you know that Meijer was founded in Greenville, Michigan?

It was founded back in 1934 by a Dutch immigrant named Hendrik Meijer. Meijer, who had previously been a local barber, got into the grocery store business during the Great Depression. His son, Frederik Meijer, was one of his first employees. Frederik went on to become the company chairman. Hendrik's grandsons, Doug and Hank Meijer, are the current co-chairmen of Meijer.

Meijer was the first grocery store to offer shopping carts and self-service shopping. Meijer also provided staple items like vinegar at low costs to attract more customers.

Meijer's store in Greenville was so successful that he opened more grocery stores in Cedar Springs and Ionia. By the 1960s, Meijer had more than 20 stores throughout West Michigan.

Today, there are 242 Meijer locations. About 50% of those are in Michigan. The rest are located in Ohio, Indiana, Kentucky, Illinois, and Wisconsin.

As of 2015, Meijer was the 26th largest retailer in America. The same year, *Forbes* magazine ranked it as No. 19 on its list of "America's Largest Private Companies."

And it all started out in Greenville, MI!

The Five-Day Work Week

Have you ever wondered who to thank for the five-day work week?

The idea came about due to the labor movement in the Detroit auto industry.

Henry Ford was the first one to offer his workers the luxury of having two days off per week.

In 1926, Ford announced the five-day workweek. He felt that Americans needed to get rid of the idea that leisure was a class privilege. Ford thought that the five-day, 40-hour work week would encourage industrial workers to vacation and shop on Saturdays.

Ford saw it as a way to stimulate the economy, as people who take part in leisure require more clothes, eat more food, and require more transportation. Many manufacturers from all around the entire *world* took his advice and began to offer the five-day work week to their employees as well.

Detroit-Style Pizza

It may come as no surprise to learn that Detroit-style pizza originated in Michigan.

It started out at Buddy's Pizza in Detroit back in the 1940s. The restaurant made the pizza at their original downtown Detroit location, prior to their expansion across the state.

Detroit-style pizza is similar to Sicilian-style pizza, which is also square in shape.

Detroit-style pizza is double-stretched, which gives it a thick but also airy square. The pizza is then topped with Wisconsin brick cheese and a drizzle of sauce.

Although you can get just about any topping on your Detroit-style pizza, the traditional pie is made with pepperoni that's tucked under the cheese. This is meant to maintain the pepperoni's flavor and prevent any charring.

Double-Baked Rye Bread

In the same way New York is known for its bagels, Michigan is known for its rye bread.

This type of rye bread was first sold at the Stage & Co. Deli during the 1950s. Invented by the deli's owner, Jack Goldberg, double-baked rye bread is different from regular rye bread. The seedless rye bread is baked 80% of the way and then baked a second time. This gives the bread a golden, crunchy crust, while leaving it softer in the middle. The rye bread is also cut thick so that it can hold deli meats and corned beef.

Jack Goldberg's invention became so popular that other delis began to sell it, too. Today, it's hard to find a deli that doesn't offer double-baked rye bread.

If you want to try out double-baked rye bread from its founders, you still can to this day. The tradition has been kept alive by the late Goldberg's son, Steven

Goldberg, who owns Stage & Co. Deli in West Bloomfield, MI.

Little Caesars Pizza

Today, it's the 3rd largest pizza chain in America, surpassed only by Pizza Hut and Domino's Pizza. But did you know that Little Caesar's started out in Michigan?

It was founded back in 1959 by Mike Ilitch and his wife Marian. They named the first store, which was located in a Garden City strip mall, "Little Caesar's Pizza Treat."

In 1962, Little Caesars sold its first franchise.

The pizza chain really began to expand during the 1980s, partly due to its slogan, "Pizza! Pizza!" The catchphrase was referring to the chain offering two pizzas for the price of one pizza by its competitors. At the time, Little Caesars served its pizza in a long package, which would include two square pizzas placed next to each other. (Since then, the company has switched to using regular pizza boxes).

By 1982, there were Little Caesars restaurants in every state in the U.S. During the 1990s and early 2000s, Little Caesars was commonplace in Kmart stores.

In 2004, Little Caesars introduced the "Hot-N-Ready," which is a large pepperoni pizza that sells for $5. It has become a permanent addition to the store's menu.

Between the years of 2008 and 2015, Little Caesars was America's fastest-growing pizza chain. By 2017, the company had more than 5,000 locations in both the U.S. and the world.

Little Caesars is headquartered in the Fox Theatre building in Downtown Detroit.

The first Little Caesar's store in Garden City closed in 2018.

RANDOM FACTS

1. Jiffy Mix is famous for its corn muffin mix. The company's first baking mix was founded by Mabel White Holmes and hit the market in 1930. The company's current CEO, Howdy Holmes, is the founder's grandson.

2. Shay Locomotives were invented by Ephraim Shay, who was a logger from Haring, Michigan. Shay patented his design in 1881. The Shay Locomotive was the most widely used locomotive there was during the late 1800s. Today, there are only 114 of the locomotives left.

3. The Packard Motor Car Company in Detroit is credited with inventing the first air-conditioned car in 1939.

4. Bell's Brewery was opened in Kalamazoo, Michigan by a Kalamazoo College alumni named Larry Bell. The brewing company is most well-known for its summer wheat ale, which is called Bell's Oberon. Bell's Cherry Stout uses cherries from Traverse City.

5. Tom's Mom's Cookies are popular throughout Michigan. The chocolate chunk cookies are made from chocolate chunks that are cut from 10-

pound chocolate bars and hand-mixed into the batter. This makes for the perfect soft/chewy cookie and the right amount of chocolate chunks. The cookies are sold in Harbor Springs and shipped throughout the country.

6. Sid Meier, who attended the University of Michigan, developed some of the most popular video game franchises of all time. Some of these include *Railroad Tycoon, Civilization,* and *Pirates!* Meier has been named the "Father of Computer Gaming."

7. The hot fudge cream puff is made with an airy pastry shell, creamy vanilla ice cream, and hot fudge. The dessert is really popular throughout Michigan. It dates back to 1875 when Fred Sanders opened the first Sanders Candy and Dessert Shops, where it was first served.

8. The Pasty was first created by the Cornish, who brought it to Michigan. The traditional meat variety is stuffed with beef, potato, rutabagas, and onions. Miniature pasties and vegetable versions are also common throughout the state. Pasties are most commonly found in the Upper Peninsula. Lawry's, which opened in 1946, is well-known for its pasties.

9. The Hummer cocktail was created at Bayview Yacht Club in Detroit. The cocktail was created by bartender Jerome Adams, who decided to

combine rum, Kahlua, and ice cream. How did it get its name? Rumor has it that someone who tasted it said it was so good that it made people want to hum. While the cocktail—and versions of the cocktail—have been sold at bars around the entire world, the drink remains popular in Michigan!

10. Chipati is a type of salad that's extremely popular in Ann Arbor, Michigan. The salad consists of lettuce, mushrooms, cheese, and peppers, which are stuffed in a thick, freshly baked pita. It's also served with a sauce that acts as both a dressing and a dip for the bread. The sauce is bright orange and creamy with a zing. Rumor has it that it's a combination of ranch dressing, hot sauce, and ketchup. Chipati was first offered at Pizza Bob's in Ann Arbor during the 1970s. The Pizza House, which opened in the mid-1980s, was famous for its Chipati.

11. Mackinac Island is famous for its fudge. In fact, a trip to the old-timey island isn't complete until you've tried some. The fudge is assembled on marble tables. The oldest fudge shop on the island is Murdick's, which dated back to the 1800s. The shop has more than 24 flavors, including Traverse City Black Cherry.

12. Detroit Street Brick is aged goat's milk cheese, which is citrus-tinged and contains green

peppercorn flecks. It was named after the brick street in front of Zingerman's in Detroit, which is where the cheese was first introduced.

13. The Cudighi is a type of sandwich that Italian immigrants brought with them to the Upper Peninsula. The sandwich features a homemade spicy Italian sausage that's generally seasoned with cinnamon and clove, marina sauce, and mozzarella cheese on a hard roll.

14. Almond boneless chicken, or Warr Shu Gai, is a popular Chinese dish in Michigan. Commonly referred to as "ABC" by Michiganders, the boneless chicken is deep-fried to crispy perfection and topped with mushroom gravy with scallions and crushed almonds. It's typically served over iceberg lettuce.

15. The Faygo brand of soda—or "pop", as it's called in Michigan—started out in Detroit. It was created by two Russian bakers named Ben and Perry Feigenson, who had the idea of turning their frosting flavors into soft drinks. The end creation was a very sweet soda with flavors that had never been invented, including Rock & Rye (a cream soda), Candy Apple, and Red Pop (a strawberry soda). The brand offers many different varieties today.

16. Bad Frog Beer was started in Rose City, Michigan. Founder Jim Wauldron first gained

recognition when he worked as a designer at a T-shirt company. After his boss told him that a frog would be too "wimpy," Wauldron designed with a frog giving a middle finger and holding a beer. Wauldron called the frog a "bad frog." People started to ask for the beer that the frog is holding in the graphic, so Wauldron learned about brewing. He opened Bad Frog Beer in 1995. Since then, the company has expanded to 25 states and other countries. Eight states have banned the beer, however, due to the frog in the logo making an obscene gesture.

17. Better Made Potato Chips started out in Detroit, Michigan. It all started out back in 1930 when Cross Moceri and Peter Cipriano bought a potato chip factory in Detroit. They named it Cross & Peters Company. In 1934, they released Better Made, their only brand of potato chips.

18. Hungry Howie's Pizza was founded by James Hearn in Taylor, Michigan back in 1973. What started out as a popular hangout for kids from the local junior high and high school turned into so much more. Within three years, the company had 65 franchise stores. Today, there are more than 550 Hungry Howie's Pizza locations, making it the 11th largest pizza chain in the USA! The pizza chain's headquarters are in Madison Heights in Metro Detroit.

19. Christian media and publishing company Zondervan was founded in 1931 in Grandville, Michigan. It was started by brothers named Bernie and Pat Zondervan. The operation originally started out in the Zondervan's farmhouse. Today, it's a part of HarperCollins Christian Publishing, Inc. Zondervan has the commercial rights to the New International Version of the Bible in North America.

20. Dart Container Corporation is the largest manufacturer of foam cups and containers in the entire world! It was first started in Mason, Michigan. In 2012, Dart purchased the Solo Cup Company.

Test Yourself – Questions

1. Which pizza chain was <u>not</u> founded in North Carolina?

   a. Domino's Pizza
   b. Pizza Hut
   c. Little Caesars Pizza

2. The three-color traffic light was invented by a Detroit-based:

   a. Chemist
   b. Pedestrian
   c. Police officer

3. The Faygo brand of soda was invented by mixing which of the following ingredients with soft drinks?

   a. Rock candy
   b. Fondant
   c. Frosting

4. Chipati is a type of:

   a. Salad
   b. Cake
   c. Cheese

5. The first employer to announce the 5-day work week was:

   a. Henry Ford
   b. Tom Monaghan
   c. Hendrik Meijer

Answers

1. b.
2. c.
3. c.
4. a.
5. a.

CHAPTER FOUR

MICHIGAN'S ATTRACTIONS

If you're planning to visit Michigan, you may be wondering what tourist attractions the state has to offer. How much do you know about the Great Lakes State's attractions?

This Island in Michigan Was the 2nd National Park in the U.S.

Did you know that Mackinac Island in Michigan was the 2nd national park? In 1875, it was originally established as Mackinac National Park. Three years earlier, Yellowstone National Park had been designated as the first national park.

Mackinac National Park drew a lot of tourism to the area. In order to accommodate the increased number of tourists, hotels were built. This included the Grand Hotel. Souvenir shops began to emerge as a way for the island's residents to make money off the tourists. A lot of wealthy people had cottages built along the island's bluffs.

Unfortunately, Mackinac National Park only lasted for 20 years. The Army proposed to abandoned Fort Mackinac, a move that would leave the park without a custodian. Michigan Governor John T. Rich requested that Congress turn the park over to the state of Michigan.

In 1895, Mackinac Island State Park opened. It was the first state-operated park in the entire country. Mackinac Island remains a state park to this day.

The island is famous due to its beautiful scenery and slow-paced way of life. Vehicles are prohibited on the island. People get around by walking, bicycle riding, and horse and buggy. There are retail shops, bars, restaurants, fudge shops, and more that are only open during the summer season, during which seasonal employees are hired.

Mackinac Island sees up to 15,000 visitors a day during the summer season.

The Grand Hotel Has Been Visited by Famous People

Today, the Grand Hotel is a major tourist attraction. While this is partly due to its history of being the film location of *Somewhere in Time*, it's also because it's a well-known fact that the hotel has seen some very famous visitors over the years.

Some of the hotel's most famous visitors include

Thomas Edison and Mark Twain. Over the years, the hotel has also been visited by several U.S. presidents. These include Harry S. Truman, John F. Kennedy, Gerald Ford, George H. W. Bush, and Bill Clinton.

The hotel, which opened in 1887, also boasts that it has the largest porch in the entire world! The porch is 660 feet long and is known for its beautiful view overlooking Lake Huron and the hotel gardens. If you aren't staying at the hotel, you'll have to pay $10 just to visit it. If you are staying, you're in for a treat. The hotel has 390 rooms and it's said that no two guest rooms are alike.

The State is Home to This Famous Museum

If you're a car fanatic, you won't want to miss out on the Henry Ford Museum.

Located in Dearborn, the museum is home to a number of exhibits and exhibits that preserve both the Ford legacy and the innovative history of inventions that have shaped the world into what it is today.

Some of the things you'll find at the museum include a replica of the 1903 Wright Flyer, vehicles that transported some of the U.S. presidents (including John F. Kennedy and Ronald Reagan), and so much more. The museum also provides an interactive experience, with exhibits like its hands-on assembly line.

You can also take the Ford Rouge Factory Tour and visit the Legacy Theater!

The Detroit Zoo Holds This Record

Did you know that the Detroit Zoo is the first zoo in America to ever have cage-less exhibits? The zoo's designer, Heinrich Hagenbeck, used moat designs to make it appear as though the animals were in their own natural habitats.

In 2005, the Detroit Zoo made history when it retired its elephants, sending them to an animal sanctuary in California.

Today, the Detroit Zoo is home to over 2,000 animals and 230 species. The zoo is most well-known for its polar bear exhibit, the Arctic Ring of Life. The exhibit, which opened in 2001, is home to two polar bears. Female polar bear, Suka, arrived at the zoo in 2018 to be paired with the zoo's male polar bear, Nuka, as part of the zoo's polar bear conservatory program. The zoo's polar bear exhibit is one of the largest in North America.

The Detroit Zoo is also famous for its National Amphibian Conservation Center. The zoo researches and makes conservative efforts for specials, such as the Wyoming toad, the Puerto Rican crested toad, and the Panamanian golden frog.

The Detroit Zoo sees more than 1.5 million visitors

every year, making it the largest paid family attraction in Michigan.

Belle Isle Park Was Designed by a Famous Landscaper

Belle Isle is the largest city island park in the United States! Encompassing 982 acres, Belle Isle Park is even larger than Central Park in New York City. Like Central Park, Belle Isle Park was designed by famous landscaper/architect Frederick Law Olmstead.

Belle Isle Park is also home to the oldest conservatory in America, the Anna Scripps Whitcomb Conservatory. The conservatory was first opened in 1904. Today, the conservatory is home to a lily pond garden, perennials, succulents, ferns, and more. The conservatory is also home to one of the largest city-owned orchid collections in the entire United States!

Michigan is Home to Five National Parks!

Did you know that Michigan is home to *five* national parks?

These national parks include:

1. **Pictured Rocks National Lakeshore** – Founded in 1966 as the United States' first national lakeshore, the park spans across more than 40 miles on the edge of Lake Superior in the Upper Peninsula. The park's name is derived from its beautiful sandstone cliffs.

2. **Sleeping Bear Dunes National Lakeshore** – Founded in 1970, this 71,000-acre park offers hiking trails, beaches, and so much more.
3. **Isle Royale National Park** – Established in 1940, the park encompasses both Isle Royale and the nearby 400-island archipelago.
4. **River Raisin National Battlefield Park** – Founded in 2010, this is the youngest national park in Michigan. Spanning across 81 acres, this park commemorates the Battle of Frenchtown during the War of 1812.
5. **Keweenaw National Historical Park** – Copper mining has taken place on the Keweenaw Peninsula for over 7,000 years, which is why it was preserved as a national historical park in 1992. The park takes up 1,700 acres of land.

Sleeping Bear Dunes National Lakeshore is Michigan's Most Visited National Park

In 2016, Michigan's national parks had over 2.5 million visitors, with Sleeping Bear Dunes National Lakeshore seeing 1.5 million visitors, making it the most visited national park in the state—and it's no wonder! The park is home to the largest freshwater sand dunes in the entire world! The park encompasses 71,200 acres of land and water. It spans across 65 miles of the Lake Michigan shoreline, as well as two islands that can be found offshore.

The dunes are beautiful and picturesque, especially when you see them with the rising or setting sun. But do you know what the federal park, which is located on Michigan's Lower Peninsula is most famous for? Its Dune Climb!

The 110-foot high wall of white sand attracts tourists from all over the country. The climb isn't for the faint-hearted. It will take your breath away!

You also won't want to miss out on the park's ghost forest. The forest was buried by moving sand dunes, only to be uncovered once the dunes shifted.

This Michigan National Park is One of the Least Visited in the Entire Country

Isle Royale National Park is the least visited park in the continental U.S. and the 3rd least visited park in the country. (It's surpassed only by Lake Clark National Park and Preserve and Gates of the Arctic National Park and Preserve, both of which are in Alaska).

There are a couple of reasons why Isle Royale National Park sees so little visitors. For starters, it's only open seasonally. The park shuts down during the winter months. The park is also less accessible than many of the other national parks throughout the country. You can't get there by car, only by ferry.

However, those who do get the opportunity to visit the park are known to spend a lot of time there. The average length of stay in Isle Royale National Park is 3.5 days, which is the highest of *any* other park in the country. The reason for this is that most people who visit the park go backpacking there.

Pictured Rocks National Lakeshore is Known for This Attraction

The Log Slide Overlook, which is located within Pictured Rocks National Lakeshore, is the national park's top attraction.

The sand dune is 300 feet high and offers spectacular views over Lake Superior and the Grand Sable Banks and Dunes.

Although the view makes Log Slide Overlook worth seeing, the real appeal comes from the trail from the overlook leading west towards the Au Sable Light Station.

As you make your way down the trail, it becomes almost level with the Lake Superior shoreline. You can easily jump off the trail and head back to the beach. It's an adventure you won't want to miss out on!

This Michigan Museum is One of the Most Visited Museums in the World

Did you know that the Detroit Institute of Arts (DIA) is one of the top six museums in America *and* one of the most visited art museums across the globe? And for good reason! With more than 100 galleries of artwork, there are over 65,000 pieces that can be found at the DIA.

The DIA's art collection contains works from ancient Egypt, medieval Europe, Africa, and so much more. It's also home to a number of famous contemporary pieces. Some of the most famous paintings that can be found at the museum include those by Vincent Van Gogh, Pablo Picasso, Georgia O'Keefe, Henri Matisse, and Rembrandt van Rijn.

As of 2014, the museum's entire collection was valued at $8.1 billion.

The Motown Museum Preserves the Record Label's History

The Motown Museum is located at "Hitsville U.S.A." (or 2648 W. Grand Boulevard, which was the record label's first headquarters). As one of Michigan's most popular tourist attractions, the museum sees thousands of visitors every year.

The museum was founded in 1985 by Esther Gordy Edwards, older sister of Berry Gordy, Jr., the founder of Motown Records.

To this day, visitors come from all over just to stand in Studio A, where some of their favorite musicians recorded their music. Where else will you get to stand exactly where the Supremes were when they recorded "Stop in the Name of Love"?

There's also a restored upper flat where Berry Gordy lived with his family early on which you can check out.

The Motown Museum is home to a number of artifacts, photographs, and other memorabilia that preserves the record label and its musicians' history and legacy. Some of the artifacts include original instruments and musical equipment, which were used between 1959 and 1972.

This is one Michigan attraction no Motown fan will want to miss out on!

Michigan is Home to These Unique Waterfalls

Did you know that the Upper Peninsula is home to Tahquamenon Falls, which are two different waterfalls with some unique features?

With their location near Lake Superior, Tahquamenon Falls is one of the U.P.'s most popular tourist attractions!

The water is known for its amber color. It's a common misconception that the water is brown due to rust or mud. The water actually gets its color from the tannins, which are leached from the trees in the swamp that gets drained by the river. The waterfalls have a drop of about 48 feet.

The river drains up to 50,000 gallons of water *per second* during the late spring. For this reason, the upper falls are the 3rd most voluminous vertical waterfall that can be found east of the Mississippi River. (They are surpassed only by Niagara Falls and Cohoes Falls in New York State).

The lower falls, which are located four miles downstream, are made of up five smaller falls. These falls cascade around an island, which you can only get to by rowboat. There's a hiking trail located on the riverside between the falls. It's common for people to play in the lower falls during the months of summer.

Walt Disney Left His Footprint on This Car Museum

When you think of Walt Disney, Michigan probably doesn't come to mind as Walt never lived in the state. But at the Gilbert Car Museum in Hickory Corners, MI, you *will* find the movie set and car from the 1967 movie *The Gnome-Mobile*.

The museum's founder, Donald Gilmore, was a good friend of Walt Disney. When the movie had finished with production, Gilmore purchased the 1930 Rolls-Royce Sedanca Deville that was used in the film. Walt Disney went to visit the Gilmore Car Museum before it officially opened and decided to give Gilmore the movie set as a gift. Both the car and movie set are still on display at the museum today.

And that's not all you'll find at the car museum! With more than 300 vintage and collector automobiles, as well as motorcycles, the museum is home to one of Michigan's largest collections of vehicles. Some of the exhibits include cars that date back to the 1890s, as well as classic cars from the 1940s, 1950s, and 1960s. You'll even find Taxi 804 from the TV series *Taxi*.

There's also the Blue Moon Diner, as well as a replica of a 1930s Shell Gas Station.

This Michigan Attraction Has Been Listed in *1,000 Places to See Before You Die*

Did you know that Frederik Meijer Gardens & Sculpture Park has been listed in *1,000 Places to See Before You Die* as one of the "30 Must-See Museums"? The botanical garden and sculpture park have earned a reputation of being one of the most culturally significant sites on the globe! *The Wall Street Journal* has compared it to the Kroller-Muller Museum and Sculpture Park in the Netherlands.

Located in Grand Rapids, the Frederik Meijer Gardens & Sculpture Park is well-known for its seasonal exhibit, *Butterflies are Blooming*. Opened from March 1st through April 30th, the temporary butterfly is the largest in the United States. The Lena Meijer Conservatory features thousands of tropical butterflies from Central America, South America, and Asia. This exhibit is the largest of Gardens, attracting more than 150,000 visitors each year.

The Gardens' *Christmas and Holiday Traditions Around the World* exhibit also draws in 75,000 visitors every year. The exhibit features food, music, and decorations from over 40 countries. There are also 30,000-holiday lights that can be seen throughout the park.

Meijer Gardens features over 170 sculptures, which includes both outdoor and indoor sculptures. One of the most famous sculptures is *The American Horse*, which was sculpted by Nina Akamu.

Some of the garden's other features include an interactive children's garden, a "Butterfly Maze", and twin waterfalls that can be found in a Japanese Garden. There's also an 1880 farmhouse, which is a replica of Lena Meijer's first house.

The Frederik Meijer Gardens & Sculpture Park is Michigan's 2nd most popular tourist attraction.

This is Michigan's Biggest Amusement Park

Located in Muskegon County, Michigan's Adventure is the largest amusement park in the Great Lakes State. Encompassing 250 acres, the park is home to 53 rides and operated by Cedar Fair. There's also the WildWater Adventure water park, which has seven roller coasters, a wooden roller coaster, and a suspended looping coaster.

It might surprise you to learn that before it became an

amusement park, it was actually opened as a petting zoo!

Established in 1956, the park was originally called Deer Park. It featured a petting zoo with—you guessed it—deer! Some of the other animals you could find at that time included llamas, chickens, ducks, and monkeys. There was also Storybook Lane, a children's recreational area.

The park's first ride was built just two years after it opened. Designed by Alan Herschell, the first ride was a 16-gauge train known as the Deer Park Special.

In 1968, Roger Jourden bought the park for $115,000. He sold off the deer and started to add attractions to the park. The first three rides were a Merry-Go-Round, a Ferris Wheel, and a Tilt-a-Whirl. Jourden renamed the park Deer Park Funland.

During the park's 20th anniversary in 1976, the Spider ride was introduced. (Eleven years later, the Spider ride went on to be sold to Michael Jackson for his Neverland Ranch).

In 1979, Deer Park Funland's first roller coaster was introduced.

In 1988, Jourden's daughter, Camille Jourden-Mark, became the park's General Manager. The park's name was also changed to Michigan's Adventure. The park added its first wooden roller coaster, as well as two live shows. In 1990, WildWater Adventure opened in order to compete with another popular water park called Pleasure Island.

The rest is history! Today, the park is the largest in Michigan and a favorite family pastime.

RANDOM FACTS

1. Binder Park Zoo in Battle Creek, MI offers a "wilderness tram" through its African Savannah exhibit.

2. Windmill Island, which is located in Holland, MI, encompasses 36 acres of gardens and Dutch architecture, including an authentic Dutch windmill that dates back to the 1760s. It's the only Dutch windmill that's ever been exported to America. It still works today.

3. The Meyer May House, which was designed by Frank Lloyd Wright and built in 1908, is located in Grand Rapids. The house is now open to visitors.

4. John Ball Zoo in Grand Rapids is known for its close encounters and interactions with animals.

5. Arch Rock is one of Mackinac Island's biggest attractions. It's a natural limestone arch that the Native Americans had many legends about . They viewed the Arch Rock as a powerful place. The limestone arch stands on the Lake Huron shoreline nearly 150 feet above the water.

6. Greenfield Village is an outdoor living history museum that's part of the Henry Ford Museum.

When Greenfield Village opened to the public in 1933, it was the first museum of its type in the entire country. Henry Ford had dozens of historic buildings transported to Dearborn, MI. When you visit the village today, you can check out Thomas Edison's Menlo Park laboratory, visit Wilbur and Orville Wright's bike shop, and get a glimpse at the first home in America to ever be wired for electricity. You can also ride a steam engine, watch an old-fashioned baseball game, and see sheep at the Firestone Farm. There's also a carousel that was built in 1913. Christmastime is a special treat at Greenfield Village, with ice skating, caroling, and so much more!

7. Rolling Hills County Park is a water park that offers fun and adventures for just about anyone! Located in Ypsilanti, MI, you'll find a wave pool, lazy river, and water slides at the park. There are also nature trails, a fishing pond, and an 18-hole golf course. During their winter, you'll find sledding, cross-country skiing, and a fireplace at The Lodge.

8. Holland State Park is one of the most visited Michigan state parks! It's well-known for its beautiful beach. You can also see the Big Red Lighthouse, which is located south of the beach.

9. Oswald's Bear Ranch, which is located in Newberry, is home to bear cubs—both rescues

and orphans. You can even have your picture taken with a bear cub!

10. There are lots of lighthouses to see in Michigan, but 40 Mile Point Lighthouse is a must-see. Located in Rogers City on the northern shore of Lake Huron, 40 Mile Point Lighthouse is conveniently located at a nearby shipwreck on the beach.

11. The Tunnel of Trees is one of Michigan's most scenic drives. Located on M-119 from Harbor Springs to Cross Village, the canopied trees are a sight to see when the area is booming with fall foliage. Even when it's not autumn, you won't want to miss out on the view along Lake Michigan.

12. Baker's Keyboard Lounge was established in 1934. It boasts itself as the World's Oldest Jazz Club.

13. Point aux Barques Lighthouse, which is located in Port Hope, is another one of the state's must-see lighthouses. Still in operation today, the lighthouse is well-known for its artifacts of Daniel J. Morrell, a ship that sank in 1966 off the coast. The 89-foot-high lighthouse offers a museum and gift shop.

14. Cross in the Woods National Shrine is located on M-68 in Indian River, Michigan. It's the largest

crucifix in the entire world. The statue of Christ has a weight of 7 tons! The cross, which is 55 feet high, was constructed from just one redwood tree. The crucifix is surrounded by a forest. The shrine was designed by sculptor Marshall Fredericks.

15. The call of the Wild Museum is located in Gaylord, MI. With an estimated 60 displays of North American animals preserved by Michigan taxidermists, the museum is also home to a wildlife discovery room and the Wildlife Theater. You'll also find Go Carts, miniature golf, and homemade items for sale.

16. The Maple Syrup Festival in Vermontville, Michigan takes place during the last weekend of April every year. Some of the things you'll find at the festival include a pancake derby and Bovine Bingo, in which you bet on a square on a football field where a cow will roam until it leaves its droppings on the winning square. Each year, a Maple Syrup Festival queen is also crowned.

17. The Lilac Festival on Mackinac Island takes place every June. The parade floats are pulled by horses, who normally pull buggies. The event is devoted to Mackinac Island's lilacs, which are typically in full bloom when the festival takes place.

18. Arcadia Bluffs is located above the shores of Lake Michigan. It's a great place to play some golf and take in the views!

19. The University of Michigan offers a number of attractions, including the Museum of Natural History.

20. The Gerald Ford Presidential Museum is the burial site and museum that commemorates the late U.S. President's life and legacy.

21. Detroit's Eastern Market features vendors that sell everything from Coney Island hot dogs to jewelry. You'll also find Motown and jazz music at Bert's Warehouse Theatre.

Test Yourself – Questions

1. Mackinac Island was almost the ___ national park in the U.S.

   a. 2nd
   b. 3rd
   c. 7th

2. The Detroit Zoo was the first zoo to:

   a. Use cageless enclosures
   b. Have a petting zoo
   c. Breed panda bears

3. The Motown Museum is most famous for:

   a. Berry Gordy's financial records
   b. The music equipment
   c. Studio A

4. Michigan's 2nd top attraction is:

   a. Mackinac Island
   b. Frederik Meijer Gardens & Sculpture Park
   c. The Henry Ford Museum

5. If you want to visit the Grand Hotel's porch and you're not a guest, you can expect to pay:

   a. $5
   b. $10
   c. $100

Answers

1. a.
2. a.
3. c.
4. b.
5. b.

CHAPTER FIVE

MICHIGAN'S SPORTS

Michigan is a state that's rich in sports history. Do you know which NBA legend or which famous boxer is from the Great Lakes State? Do you know which legendary NFL quarterback started out his football career at the University of Michigan? Read on to find out the answers to these and other sports about Michigan sports!

This Boxing Legend is From Michigan

Did you know that Floyd Mayweather Jr. was born and raised in Grand Rapids, Michigan?

Floyd Jr. wasn't the first member of his family to become a boxer. His father, Floyd Mayweather Sr., was a former professional boxer who gained a lot of fame for fighting the notorious Sugar Ray Leonard. Floyd Mayweather Sr.'s brothers, Jeff Mayweather and Roger Mayweather, were also pro boxers. Roger Mayweather, who won two world championships, was Floyd Mayweather Jr.'s trainer. As a result, Floyd Jr. never really considered a career besides boxing.

Floyd Jr. had a rough life. His mother was a drug addict, and he had a rocky relationship with his father. Floyd has said that his father only spent time with him when he took him to the gym or work on his boxing. His father whipped him frequently and also sold drugs to support the family. His father eventually was incarcerated, which further strained their relationship.

Floyd Mayweather Jr. went to Ottawa Hills High School before he dropped out. He made the decision to support his mom and earning a living with boxing felt more important than school.

And earn a living, he did. Floyd Mayweather Jr. competed from 1996 to 2007 and again from 2009 to 2015. He also competed in one fight in 2017. Over the course of his career, Mayweather held world titles in five weight classes, as well as the lineal championship in four weight classes. Mayweather retired with an undefeated record.

Mayweather is considered to be the best defensive boxer in history. He's also thought to be the most accurate punchers of all-time. He holds the record for 26 consecutive wins in world title fights.

In addition, Floyd Jr. is one of the most lucrative all-time pay-per-view attractions, in regards to any sport.

In 2014 and 2015, *Forbes* listed Floyd Mayweather Jr. as the No. 1 highest-paid athlete in the entire world. And it all started out in Grand Rapids, MI!

This Famous Former MLB Pitcher is From Michigan

Did you know that former MLB pitcher Jim Abbott was born and raised in Flint, Michigan? Abbott is famous for being a pitcher, even though he was born without a right hand!

Jim Abbott graduated from Flint Central High School, where he was a successful pitcher and quarterback.

He later went on to attend the University of Michigan, where he won the James E. Sullivan Award as the best amateur athlete in the country in 1987. Abbott was the first baseball player to ever win the award. During the three years he played for Michigan, he led them to two Big Ten championships.

Abbott also won the United States an unofficial gold medal in the 1988 Summer Olympics, for which baseball was a demonstration sport.

In the 1988 draft, the California Angels selected Jim Abbott 8th overall.

Abbott later, and most famously, played for the New York Yankees. During the 1993 season, Abbott threw a no-hitter against the Cleveland Indians. The same year, Abbott starred as himself in Episode 9 of Season 1 of *Boy Meets World*.

Over the course of his 10-year career, Abbott played for the California Angels, the New York Yankees, the Chicago White Sox, and the Milwaukee Brewers.

In 2007, Abbott was elected to the College Baseball Hall of Fame.

At the time of his retirement in 1999, Jim Abbott had amassed a career record of 87 wins, 108 losses and a 4.25 earned run average.

This Olympian Attended the University of Michigan

Did you know that competitive swimmer Michael Phelps once attended the University of Michigan? It might surprise you to learn that his reason for attending the university was *not* for educational purposes!

Beginning from the age of 11, Phelps was trained by Bob Bowman. Phelps has compared Bowman to a drill sergeant due to his disciplined and regimented style of training. After the 2004 Summer Olympics, in which Phelps competed, Bowman became the head swim coach at the University of Michigan.

Phelps followed Bowman to the University of Michigan to train under him. Although he took classes so that he could train, Phelps didn't work towards a degree at the university. Phelps also acted as a voluntary assistant coach for the Wolverines.

Following the 2008 Summer Olympics, Bowman went back to Baltimore and Phelps followed him to continue training under him. He later followed him to Arizona as well.

Michael Phelps is considered the most decorated and most successful Olympian in history. With 23 Olympic gold medals, Phelps holds the record for the most all-time Olympic gold medals.

This Legendary NFL Quarterback Struggled While Playing for the University of Michigan

Today, he's considered one of the greatest quarterbacks of all-time. He's won six Super Bowls, which is more than any NFL player in history! But did you know that before Tom Brady played for the New England Patriots, he struggled while playing for the University of Michigan?

Tom Brady played for the University of Michigan Wolverines between the years of 1995 and 1999. It might surprise you to learn that he was a backup quarterback during his freshman and sophomore years. In fact, he had a hard time getting playing time and even saw a sports psychologist to help him cope with the frustration and anxiety he experienced due to this challenge. At one point, Brady even considered transferring.

Brady worked with Greg Harden, who was the University of Michigan's assistant athletic director. The two met weekly and worked on Brady's confidence in order to improve his performance while on the field.

During his junior and senior years, Brady was the starter for every game. He also set a new record for the Wolverines for the most completions and pass attempts in a single season, with a total of 214. With Brady as a starter, the Wolverines won 20 games and lost 5. During his junior year, Brady also set a school record for completions in a 31 to 16 loss against Ohio State. The same year, the University of Michigan defeated the University of Arkansas in the Citrus Bowl, with a score of 45 to 31.

Brady wasn't drafted by the New England Patriots until the 6th round in the NFL Draft in 2000. Since he was selected so late, many consider Brady to be the biggest "steal" in the history of the NFL Draft.

In addition to leading the Patriots to win six Super Bowls, Brady has led the Patriots to more division titles than any other NFL quarterback in history.

As of 2018, Tom Brady held the following records:

- No. 1 in playoff wins and appearances for any player in the NFL

- No. 3 in career touchdown passes
- No. 4 in career passing yards for a regular season
- No. 4 in career presser rating
- The first and only quarterback to ever reach 200 regular season wins
- The quarterback with the most wins in NFL history

In addition, Brady also tied with Wes Welker for the longest touchdown pass at 99 yards.

And to think that Brady had to fight for playtime during his first two years with the University of Michigan!

The Detroit Tigers Weren't Named for Their Socks

A lot of MLB fans believe that the Detroit Tigers were named after the orange-striped socks they wear.

This is incorrect.

Although the team did have one red stripe on their uniform socks when the team was named back in 1901, their socks have nothing to do with where "Tigers" came from.

During the 19th century, there were military units in Detroit and throughout other areas of Michigan that had been given the nickname of "tigers" due to how fiercely they thought. One such example is the

Detroit Light Guard unit, which had been called the "Fighting Tigers." Detroit's first franchise for the National League of baseball was first known as the Wolverines and then, later, the Tigers. So, when the American League franchise was started in 1901, they adopted the name the "Tigers."

It wasn't until 1927—or 26 years *after* the team had already gotten its name—that the Tigers began to wear orange-striped socks with their baseball uniforms.

This Legendary NBA Player is From Michigan

Did you know that Magic Johnson is from Michigan?

Magic, whose real name is Earvin Johnson Jr., was born in Lansing, MI.

Johnson developed a fondness of basketball at a young age. He idolized player Bill Russell, along with Earl Monroe and Marques Haynes. Johnson learned the game from his father, who played high school basketball. His mom and her brothers had also played basketball as kids.

Johnson knew by 8th grade that he wanted to become a professional basketball player. In junior high, he played for the basketball team and once scored 48 points in a game.

Johnson had been excited to play basketball at Sexton High School, which had a good basketball team and was a predominantly black school. However, the district ended up busing him to Everett High School, which was a predominantly white school where racism ran rampant. His brother Larry was kicked off the basketball team due to a confrontation during practice. Even though Larry begged Earvin not to join the team, he did. Unfortunately, he didn't have a good experience, with his teammates not passing the ball to him. He also nearly fought another student, but the head coach prevented it from happening. Earvin didn't quit the team, however. He accepted the situation and became a leader to the small group of other black kids who were also on the team.

Years later, Johnson said his experience at Everett helped teach him how to understand white people. He says it was one of the best things that ever happened to him.

It was during his sophomore year playing basketball at Everett High School where Johnson earned his famous nickname "Magic." He recorded a triple-double of 36 points, 18 rebounds, and 16 assists. The nickname was given to him to *Lansing State Journal* sports writer Fred Stabley Jr. Magic's mother, who was a Christian, didn't approve of the nickname, believing it was sacrilegious.

During his senior year, Magic Johnson led Everett High School to 27 wins, with only 1 loss. Under his lead, the team also won the state championship game.

Magic Johnson was chosen first in the 1979 NBA draft by the Los Angeles Lakers. At the time, Johnson was considered to be the best high school player of any sport to ever come out of the state of Michigan.

During his rookie season, Magic Johnson won a championship and an NBA Finals Most Valuable Players Award. He went on to win four more championships during his time with the Lakers.

Over the course of his career, Johnson became the NBA's all-time leader in average assists per game and won an Olympic gold medal as a member of the 1992 U.S. men's Olympic basketball team. Today, he's recognized as one of the greatest NBA players of all-time and was inducted into the Basketball Hall of Fame.

Magic Johnson retired from the NBA in 1991 after he announced his diagnosis of HIV. He played in the 1992 All-Star Game and won the All-Star MVP Award, but his teammates protested and he retired again until 1996 when he came back to play 32 more games.

Michigan State University's Mascot is Iconic

Did you know that the Michigan State University mascot is one of the most iconic and well-known mascots in college sports?

The mascot, "Sparty" the Spartan, is a muscular male Spartan warrior. Sparty wears Greek armor and an

Imperial-style Roman legionary helmet. The mascot costume is worn by an anonymous student at athletic events and other university functions.

Although it's often rumored that the student who plays Sparty receives financial compensation or a scholarship, it's actually a volunteer. Tryouts are held every year to choose the student who will portray Sparty.

Sparty is often ranked at the top of college mascot lists, which is probably due to his beloved personality. Sparty is known to entertain the crowd with his antics. He's often lifted on the cheerleaders' shoulders and often does one-handed push-ups. Sparty first gained fame during the '90s when he was featured carrying injured gymnast Kerri Strug in a TV ad that promoted ESPN's *SportsCenter*.

Sparty has won a number of titles, including *Muscle and Fitness* magazine's "Buffest Mascot" and the Universal Cheer Association/Universal Dance Association College Nationals' Best Mascot National Championship. The mascot was also featured on the Wii's *NCAA Football 09*, which was the first time someone other than an athlete had ever appeared on it.

At one point, Sparty was even on a series of Jones Soda bottles in the 2000s!

Although Sparty is most well-known in mascot form,

there's also a Sparty statue! The original Sparty statue was designed by art professor Leonard D. Jungwirth back in 1943. The statue had to be cast in terra cotta due to World War II rationing. In 2005, Jungwirth's design was replaced with a bronze replica. The original statue was moved inside to keep it safe from harsh weather conditions.

This Legendary MLB Player *Almost* Became the Detroit Tigers' Manager

Did you know that Babe Ruth *almost* became manager of the Detroit Tigers at one point?

So, what prevented it from happening? Babe Ruth had been vacationing in Hawaii.

It was during the 1933/1934 season that Tigers' team owner Frank Navin knew he was in need of a winning team manager. Navin had a talented team of players, including Charlie Gehringer and Hank Greenberg, but the New York Yankees were still on top.

Navin knew that Babe Ruth was about to leave the Yankees, so Frank offered the team money to acquire the rights to the legendary player. Ruth, it turns out, had aspirations of becoming a team manager.

However, Ruth was vacationing in Honolulu at the time, preventing Navin from being able to meet with him. Instead, Mickey Cochrane became the Tigers' manager.

It turned out to be a great decision. During Cochrane's first two years, the Tigers won two pennants. They also won the 1935 World Series.

This Detroit Lions Player Holds Several NFL Records

Did you know that Detroit Lions player Matthew Stafford has set several NFL records?

Stafford has accomplished the following:

- He's the 4th quarterback in the history of the NFL who has ever thrown more than 5,000 yards in a single season. Stafford was one of three players who accomplished this feat during the 2011 football season.
- Stafford is the faster player in NFL history. He's the first and only player who has ever reached 30,000 yards over the course of 109 games.
- Matthew Stafford accomplished eight comeback wins in 2016, making him the NFL player with the most comeback wins in a single season.
- The $135 million extension he signed with the Lions in 2017 made him the highest paid NFL player in history at the time of the contract.

This Figure Skater is From Michigan

Did you know that figure skater Evan Bates is from Michigan?

Bates, who was born in Ann Arbor, attended Horn High School and the University of Michigan.

He began skating when he was four years old, training as a single skater. He trained under ice dancing coaches Yaroslava Nechaeva and Yuri Chesnichenko.

Today, Bates and his skating partner, Madison Chock, have won two World medals (silver and bronze), two Grand Prix Final silver medals, and the 2015 U.S. national champion and the 2019 Four Continents champion titles. In 2014 and 2018, Bates and Chock represented the United States in the Winter Olympics.

This Former Detroit Tigers Player is Regarded as One of the Best MLB Players of All Time

Did you know that one of the best MLB players of all-time once played for the Detroit Tigers?

Tyrus "The Georgie Peach" Cobb was an outfielder who spent 22 seasons of his MLB career with the Detroit Tigers. During the last six seasons he spent with the Tigers, Cobb was the team's player/manager. He retired from the MLB while playing for the Philadelphia Athletics.

Over the course of his career, Cobb set 90 MLB records. His combined total of 4,065 runs scored and runs batted in remains, to this day, the highest to ever be produced by any major league player in history.

As of 2018, Ty Cobb still holds the records for the following:

- The highest career batting average
- The most career batting titles
- The highest number of home steals
- The highest number of second base, third base, and home steals in succession
- The youngest player in MLB history to score 2,000 runs and amass 4,000 hits

Additionally, Ty Cobb ranks No. 5 in all-time number of games played.

In 1936, Cobb received 222 inaugural ballot votes to be inducted into the Baseball Hall of Fame, which was more than any other player in history until Tom Seaver in 1992.

Sporting News magazine placed Cobb at No. 3 on their list of "Baseball's 100 Greatest Players."

The Detroit Red Wings Have Set This NHL Record

Did you know that, as of 2018, the Detroit Red Wings have won the most Stanley Cup championships out of any NHL team? The team is also 3rd overall in terms of how often they've played in Stanley Cup championships, surpassed only by the Montreal Canadiens and the Toronto Maple Leafs.

The Detroit Red Wings have won the Stanley Cup 11 times total. They won the cup during the following years:

- 1936
- 1937
- 1943
- 1950
- 1952
- 1954
- 1955
- 1997
- 1998
- 2002
- 2008

In addition, the Red Wings have won 2,858 all-time regular season games.

Michigan is the Birthplace of...

Snowboarding! Well, *technically*. The precursor to the modern-day snowboard started out in Michigan.

Back in 1965, an engineer named Sherman Poppen designed a toy for his daughters. He tied two skis together and attached a rope at one end that would allow them to steer as they stood on the board and went downhill.

Poppen's wife came up with the name for his invention: the "snurfer" (which is a combination of "snow" and "surfer").

Poppen's invention quickly gained popularity. In 1968, the first snurfer racing competition was held in Muskegon. There were more than 200 people in the audience. These competitions continued into the late 1970s.

By 1998, snowboarding was included in the Winter Olympics.

This Competitive Snowboarder Hails from Michigan

Competitive snowboarder Nick Baumgartner is from Iron River, Michigan!

Baumgartner won the gold and silver medals in the 2011 and 2012 Winter X Games. The Winter X Games are an extreme sporting event that's hosted by ESPN.

Additionally, Baumgartner competed in the 2014 Winter Olympics. He was placed in the snowboard cross A team, but unfortunately, had a poor start to the race and placed No. 4. (Only the top 3 competitors advanced to the quarterfinals).

Baumgartner is a graduate of West Iron County High School!

Detroit is Known as "Hockeytown"

Did you know that Detroit has earned the famous nickname of "Hockeytown"?

This is thanks to the city's avid hockey fans. The nickname was—and continues to be—so widely used by sports commentators and hockey fans in Detroit that the city's NHL team even decided to trademark it!

The term "Hockeytown," when used in combination with a winged wheel logo, is a trademark owned by the Detroit Red Wings.

RANDOM FACTS

1. Serena Williams' life started out in Michigan! Though the family moved to Compton, California when she was very young, Williams was born in Saginaw, MI.

2. Detroit has bid on hosting the Summer Olympics more times than any other city that has not yet hosted. It still hasn't hosted them yet.

3. The Detroit Tigers have won the World Series on four occasions: in 1935, 1945, 1968, and, most recently, in 1984.

4. The Detroit Lions are one of only four NFL teams that have never made it to the Super Bowl. (The other three NFL teams that have never played in the Super Bowl are the Cleveland Browns, the Jacksonville Jaguars, and the Houston Texans).

5. The Detroit Lions chose their name because of the Detroit Tigers.

6. The Detroit Red Wings' team name has changed three times. When the team was first founded in 1926, it was called the Detroit Cougars. The NHL team was renamed the Detroit Falcons in 1930. Two years later, it was renamed the Detroit Red Wings, which it remains today.

7. The Red Wings used to play their home games at Joe Louis Arena (1979-2017), but they moved to the new Little Caesars Arena for the 2017-2018 hockey season.

8. The University of Michigan's mascot is the Wolverine, but not in the way you might think. The university's mascot doesn't appear at sporting events. The athletic department doesn't allow the mascot to be used in this way. That being said, U of Michigan students have been referring to themselves as the "Wolverines" since 1861.

9. The University of Michigan's "winged helmet" was first designed in 1938, when it was stitched into cow-hide helmets. The helmet design has evolved. Although it was originally meant to help halfbacks spot receivers downfield, it's now a popular part of the U of Michigan's varsity teams and has been adopted by other college teams.

10. The University of Michigan's football stadium is known as "The Big House." The stadium is one of the largest football stadiums in the country. It can seat up to 100,000 people.

11. Ohio State is one of Michigan State's biggest rivals. As of 2018, Michigan has beaten Ohio State 15 times... and lost 31 times. The Spartans

did beat the Buckeyes the first three games they have ever played, however (in 1912, 1951, and 1953).

12. Former NFL player Tony Dungy was born in Jackson, Michigan. Dungy played for the Pittsburgh Steelers, San Francisco 49ers, and the New York Giants.

13. NBA player Draymond Green is from Saginaw, Michigan. Green has played for the Golden State Warriors since 2012.

14. NBA player Devin Booker is from Grand Rapids, Michigan. Booker, who has played for the Phoenix Suns since the start of his NBA career, was the youngest player to score 60 points in a game when he finished with 70 points against the Boston Celtics in 2017. Devin Booker's father, Melvin Booker, also played professional basketball.

15. Women's ice hockey player Megan Keller was born in Farmington, Michigan. She plays for the Boston College Eagles in the NCAA competition. Keller also played in the U.S.A. Women's 2018 Olympic Team.

16. Former MLB player Barry Larkin played baseball for the University of Michigan. Regarded as one of the top players of his era, Larkin went on to play for the Cincinnati Reds.

17. The Bayview Mackinac Boat Race is one of the largest fresh-water boat races in the entire world, with more than 200 boats entering every year.

18. Former NFL player Desmond played football for the University of Michigan. The Heisman Trophy winner went on to play for several teams, beginning his NFL career with the Washington Redskins and ending it with the Detroit Lions.

19. Former NBA player Cazzie Russell started out his career playing basketball for the University of Michigan. Russell went on to become an NBA All-Star and played for several teams, including the New York Knicks, Golden State Warriors, and Los Angeles Lakers.

20. Former NBA player Glen Rice played basketball for the University of Michigan. Rice went on to play for several teams, including the Miami Heat, Charlotte Hornets, Los Angeles Lakers, and New York Knicks. His achievements include being a three-time NBA All-Star and winning the NCAA and the NBA championships.

Test Yourself – Questions

1. The name of the Michigan State University mascot is:

   a. Sparky
   b. Sparty
   c. Spartan

2. Which famous athlete did _not_ attend Michigan state?

   a. Tom Brady
   b. Michael Phelps
   c. Derek Jeter

3. Detroit is known as:

   a. Hockeytown
   b. Baseball Town
   c. Football Town

4. The Detroit Tigers were once almost owned by:

   a. A-Rod
   b. Jackie Robinson
   c. Babe Ruth

5. The precursor to the modern-day snowboard was the _____.

   a. Surfer
   b. Snurfer
   c. Mountainboard

Answers

1. b.

2. c.

3. a.

4. c.

5. b.

CHAPTER SIX

MICHIGAN'S URBAN LEGENDS, UNSOLVED MYSTERIES, AND OTHER WEIRD FACTS!

Every state has its fair share of unusual occurrences, unsolved mysteries, and locations that are believed to be haunted. Michigan is a state that's booming with unsolved mysteries and haunted locales. It's also home to a few folklores. Do you know about the Michigan Dogman? Have you heard about the creepy monster, which Detroit now celebrates each year in the form of a parade? Have you heard of the Michigan Triangle? This chapter will be filled with creepy things. It might scare you a little. It might leave you with goosebumps. Read on at your own discretion!

The Michigan Dogman

The Dogman is generally described as a large dog that's able to stand upright or, in some versions of the legend, a human body with a dog head. The legendary beast has been spotted in many states through America, including Michigan. In fact, sightings of the Dogman have allegedly been taking place in Michigan's Lower Peninsula since the late 1800s.

The earliest known Dogman sighting took place in Wexford county in 1887 when several lumberjacks allegedly chased the creature into a hollow log. Thinking the beast was a regular dog, one of the lumberjacks used a stick to try to get it out of the log. The lumberjacks claimed to hear a loud scream and the Dogman jumped out of the log, scaring them away.

In 1987, Steve Cook, a radio DJ at WTCM-FM in Traverse City, released a song about the Dogman. While the song was originally meant to be a joke, radio listeners called in to share their encounters with the creature. One of the callers was an elderly man named Robert Fortney, who reported an alleged sighting of the Dogman in the 1930s. Fortney claimed to be fishing in a river near Paris, Michigan when he saw a pack of wild dogs come out of the woods. He was able to scare off most of the dogs with a warning gunshot, but one of the dogs stayed behind. Fortney said that the dog, which was black with blue eyes, stood on its hind legs and gave him an intimidating stare. Fortney says he shot the dog, which ran back into the woods.

Although there have been numerous alleged Dogman sightings reported in Michigan over the years, no physical evidence of the Dogman has ever been found.

The Melon Heads

The Melon Heads of Michigan's Lower Peninsula are believed to live in forested areas throughout the state. The Melon Heads are believed to be children who were born with hydrocephalus, which causes liquid around the brain and head enlargement.

There are other theories on what the Melon Heads actually are. According to legend, the Melon Heads in Allegan County had once been in the Junction Insane Asylum following World War II. It's believed that medical researchers did cruel experiments that resulted in their large heads. The children were thought to be released or may have escaped into the woods. After inbreeding with one another, the mutant children were thought to attack and eat any animal or human that crossed their paths.

The ruins of the old Junction Insane Asylum are thought to be on the property of Felt Mansion. People have reported hearing strange noises and odd silhouettes on the property. However, the Allegan County Historical Society has maintained that the insane asylum never existed.

It's possible that the legend of the Melon Heads may have originated when Felt Mansion was the St. Augustine Seminary. Some locals called the St. Augustine Seminary students "melon heads" because it was a private school. There was also some stigma against the school and its students due to religious differences.

Even though it seems safe to say that the Melon Heads are nothing but an urban legend, there are still alleged reports of them in recent years.

The Michigan Triangle

Did you know that Michigan is home to its own Bermuda Triangle?

Many ships and planes have disappeared over the triangle, which spans over Lake Michigan. The triangle can be formed by drawing a triangle from three locations: Benton Harbor, Michigan, Ludington, Michigan, and Manitowoc, Wisconsin.

The Michigan Triangle, which is sometimes called the Lake Michigan Triangle, has been at the forefront of a number of strange and unexplained incidents, including shipwrecks, missing planes, and even UFO sightings.

One of the most well-known and eerie tales about the Michigan Triangle is the disappearance of Captain George Donner of the O.M. McFarland. Back in 1937,

Captain Donner went missing from his cabin while the ship was in the Michigan Triangle. His cabin had been locked from the inside. The crew searched for their captain, but there was no sign of him or what might have happened to him. Donner was never seen again.

Then, in 1950, Northwest Flight 2501 disappeared over the Michigan Triangle. The Northwest Airlines plane, which was carrying 58 people, was the worst aviation accident in U.S. history at the time. The eeriest part about it was that the plane was never found.

Lake Michigan is known for its squalls, with winds frequently reaching up to 75 mph. Some experts believe that this could explain some of the strange incidents that have happened over the lake. However, squalls haven't been the cause of some of the incidents, leading many to believe that the triangle is the result of supernatural causes.

The Strange Disappearance of Connie Converse

Back in the 1950s, Connie Converse was a folk singer who was popular in New York City's Greenwich Village.

Converse didn't ever rise to fame, however. She played at bars and parties, but she never recorded a studio album. The only recordings of Converse's music were done on a tape recorder.

Converse appeared on *The Morning Show* with Walter Cronkite in 1954. Shortly thereafter, other musicians, including Bob Dylan, had risen to fame, while her career wasn't taking off.

By 1961, Converse had given up on trying to make a career in the music industry. She moved to Ann Arbor, Michigan, to be near her family. There, she worked as a secretary and as an editor for an academic journal.

However, Converse became very depressed. She became a heavy drinker and smoker.

During the summer of 1974, Converse abruptly left Michigan, without telling anyone where she was going. She did pack up her things, and she did send letters to her friends and family to inform them of her desire to start a new life somewhere else.

Her communications eventually stopped, however. After years had gone by without any contact from her, Converse's family grew afraid of her wellbeing.

A few years after Connie's disappearance, people claimed to see a listing for someone with her name in either Kansas or Oklahoma. During the 1980s, her brother Phillip hired a detective to look for his sister. However, the investigator wasn't able to turn up anything. The private investigator also told the family that even *if* he was able to track her down, it was her right to leave. Her family stopped looking for her at that time.

Phillip suspected that Connie committed suicide. He believed that she had driven her car into a body of water. This seemed possible due to her depression.

Since her disappearance and due to the mystery surrounding it, Converse has gained a cult following. Old recordings by the musician have been tracked down, and people have come up with their own theories about what happened to the musician.

In 2014, the film *We Lived Alone: The Connie Converse Documentary* was released.

The Unsolved Murder of Chelsea Bruck

In October of 2014, Chelsea Bruck drove with her friend to a Halloween party that took place in Frenchtown Township. Bruck had dressed up as Poison Ivy from *Batman*.

The party had received a lot of social media attention, drawing in more than 700 people from Michigan and other states.

At approximately 3 a.m., Bruck was seen outside talking to a man who had dark hair, a light mustache, and black-framed glasses.

That was the last time anyone would ever see Bruck again.

Over the course of the next few days, investigators and volunteers searched for Chelsea. A million missing person posters were distributed across the entire U.S.

Due to how many costumed people there were at the party, no one was able to identify the mystery man Bruck is believed to have left the party with.

In April of 2015, Bruck's Poison Ivy costume was located at an abandoned construction site a few miles away from where the party had taken place. Three weeks later, her body was found.

To date, the killer hasn't been found.

The Haunted Grand Hotel

The Grand Hotel may be Mackinac Island's top attraction, but did you know that it's believed to be haunted?

According to local lore, construction workers who were digging the hotel's foundation found so many skeletons that they weren't even able to count them all. It has been said that the workers stopped trying to collect all of the bones and simply built the hotel over them. So, it's no surprise that people believe the hotel to be haunted.

One of the eeriest stories about the old hotel is the "black mass." Two maintenance workers were checking out the hotel's theater stage when one of them was overtaken by a strange feeling that something was watching them. The only word he could think to describe it was "evil." When he looked out over the theater, there were two glowing red eyes in the shadows. The black mass charged him, knocking him off his feet. The man allegedly woke up two days later at a hospital and vowed to never return to the hotel.

Since then, a number of odd occurrences have been reported at the old hotel. Staff members have claimed to see the apparition of a man in a top hat sitting at the 2nd floor's bar piano, who disappears and leaves behind the scent of cigar smoke. There have also been reported sightings of a Victorian-era woman who roams the hotel's employee housing. The ghost is said to even curl up next to workers at nighttime.

The Ghost of Mission Point Resort

Mission Point Resort on Mackinac Island is also thought to be haunted.

The resort was originally built during the 1950s as a world conference center for the Moral Re-Alignment, which was a cult-like religious group. The property was sold a few times before it eventually became the Mission Point Resort.

Today, the resort is considered to be one of the most haunted spots on Mackinac Island (which is saying a lot, since Mackinac Island is believed to have quite a few haunted locations).

For starters, there's the resort's resident ghost Harvey. The ghost is said to linger in the Mission Point theater, often pinching and poking young women in the dark.

Harvey is thought to be a student who died in the late 1960s. According to legends, Harvey was a brokenhearted guy who went to the bluffs located behind the resort and shot himself. Harvey's body allegedly wasn't found for six months.

However, not everyone believes this version of the story. Todd Clements, a local paranormal investigator/historian, thinks there may have been someone else involved in Harvey's death. The student's death was ruled a suicide, but there were *two* bullets to his head and the gun wasn't anywhere near his body. Clements thinks Harvey has unfinished business and that's why his spirit still haunts the island.

Harvey's not the only spirit that's thought to haunt the resort. There's also believed to be a young girl who calls out for her parents. There are also thought to be Native American spirits that wander the property of the resort.

The Mission Point Resort is so notoriously haunted that it even attracted SyFy's *Ghost Hunters* back in

2010.

The Unsolved Murder of Donald Goines

The murder of Donald Goines is one of the most chilling unsolved mysteries to take place in the state of Michigan.

Donald Goines, who was a high school dropout, joined the U.S. Air Force during the Korean War. Goines, who had lied about his age, was given an honorable discharge at 17 years old. When he returned to Michigan, Goines became addicted to drugs and became involved in street crime.

Goines spent the 1960s in and out of jail for his crimes. In 1969, however, he decided to become a writer. Though he originally planned to write Westerns, he decided on urban/crime novels, instead. While he was serving time at Jackson Penitentiary for attempted larceny charges, Goines wrote his first novel, *Whoreson*. The novel was accepted for publication.

Once he had been released from jail, Goines stopped committing crimes, but he couldn't kick his heroin addiction. To pay for his drugs, he continued to write. He wrote 16 novels over the course of four years. His publisher decided to publish a few of his novels, including the *Kenyatta* series, under the pseudonym "AI C. Clark."

In October of 1974, the police received an anonymous call that Donald Goines and his common-law wife, Shirley Sailor, were dead. Goines was found dead in the living room of his Highland Park, Michigan apartment, while Sailor's body was found in the kitchen. Both of them had been shot in the head and chest. Goines' two children were found alive in the basement.

None of Goines' neighbors had heard the shooting take place.

To this day, it's unknown who shot Donald Goines and Shirley Sailor and why.

Several theories abound. It's thought that Goines may have been killed over a drug debt. Another popular theory is that Goines may have angered someone with his novels, which were known to be based on real criminals who he had encountered.

The Michigan Lake Monster

Did you know that Michigan is believed to have its own lake monster?

The monster, who is believed to be similar to the Lochness monster, is known as "Pressie." Sometimes referred to as the Lake Superior Serpent, Pressie is said to live in the Presque Isle River where it meets Lake Superior.

The monster has been described as a long-necked, serpent-like creature with a large jaw.

There have been several reported sightings of the monster over the years. In 1977, a couple photographed what they believed to be a giant serpent in the lake. Unfortunately, the photo turned out to be too blurry to determine what it was of. Then in 1981, a group of kids in Munising reported seeing a huge serpent with high humps jump in the water. In the 1990s, a fisherman claimed to see Pressie drag a deer under the water, leaving nothing behind but the animal's severed head.

There haven't been any reports of Pressie since the 1990s, but many believe the monster is still out there, lurking in the depths of the river!

UFOs Have Been Spotted in Michigan

While Michigan does not rank on the top 10 states with UFO sightings, there have been numerous reports of unidentified flying objects in the state. Back in 1966, a swarm of UFOs was spotted.

On March 20th, 1966, a man named Frank Mannor watched as a pyramid-shaped UFO landed in a swamp near his home in Dexter Township. Mannor and his son, Ron, went to investigate the object. When they reached the swamp, they saw the UFO there. It was flashing red and white lights.

Authorities were contacted and went to check out the situation. When they located the UFO, it quickly took off into the sky. The police officers called for help, gathering a team of 40 more police and local volunteers.

As the officers continued to check out the swamp area, a few people saw flashing bright lights in the sky. One of the police also reported seeing a UFO that was blueish in color fly over his car.

The search team reportedly saw the first UFO being followed by three other UFOs.

During the days that followed, there were reported sightings of UFOs and strange, unexplained flashing lights across the entire state.

All of the reported sightings drew the attention of Congressman Weston Vivian. Dr. J. Allen Hynek, an astronomer/UFO investigator, was sent to Michigan by the U.S. Air Force.

Hynek spoke to witnesses for a couple of days before announcing at a conference held in Detroit that the "UFOs" and "flashing lights" were probably actually the result of swamp gas.

Hynek's explanation caused many Michigan citizens to be outraged. Newspapers felt that it was all a cover-up. Then Congressman Gerald Ford insisted that Congress organize an investigation.

Although the UFO sightings were never explained as anything other than swamp gas, one thing was...

well, *strange*.

Samples taken from the ground and water near where Frank Mannor and his son first spotted the UFO showed that the radiation levels were higher than normal. No explanation was ever given for this.

The Strange Murder of Lydia Thompson

Lydia Thompson, who was from Russia, married a British man named Louis. When the two settled in Detroit after World War I, Louis opened a car dealership. They also owned a laundromat, which Lydia managed.

After years of success and riches, Lydia suspected that Louis was having an affair. She hired some private investigators to follow Louis and learned that he was having an affair with a secretary named Helen Budnik.

Although Lydia wanted to try to fix their marriage, Louis ended up moving out of the house and divorced her.

In October of 1945, Lydia Thompson was found dead in a marsh near Pontiac, Michigan. She had been tortured and stabbed with an ice pick. Her head had been decapitated.

While authorities initially suspected Louis and Helen of the murder, they both passed a polygraph. They also had good alibis around the time of the murder.

Over a year later, Louis and Helen were arrested and charged with Lydia's murder.

Although there wasn't much evidence against them, what was believed to be a breakthrough happened when a woman came forward and said her boyfriend had confessed to killing Lydia. The woman said her boyfriend had claimed that Louis had paid him $10,000 to kill Lydia Thompson.

In a turn of events, the suspected killer was married and had come up with the story to scare his girlfriend away.

Without any other evidence linking them to the crime, Louis and Helen were released.

To date, the murder remains a mystery.

Many people believed that the couple was actually guilty. However, there's another theory about who had killed Lydia. It was thought that one of the private investigators she had hired to catch her husband cheating may have killed her.

During the months prior to her death, Lydia had been acting strangely. She had bought herself a gun and told her friends that someone was following her. Her friends had told her she was being paranoid.

Louis had also loaned Lydia $7,000 during the year she had died, even though she was well-off due to her laundromat.

Investigators were never able to determine where the money had gone. It was thought that she may have used the money to pay the detectives.

However, a popular theory is that Lydia had used the money to pay someone to kill Helen Budnik. After taking the money, it's believed that the hitman had killed Helen, instead.

Plymouth Township's "John Doe"

The "John Doe" of Plymouth Township is one of the area's biggest unsolved mysteries.

In May of 1997, a man who was surveying the woods in Plymouth Township spotted a mouse as it scampered into a rolled-up carpet. The man lifted the carpet in order to catch the mouse and discovered a human skeleton underneath of it.

It was determined that the skeleton was that of a white man between 35 and 50 years old. The man was wearing a blue-and-white striped shirt, blue shorts, and socks related to the 1980 Olympics.

Autopsy reports showed that the unidentified man had been killed by a blow to the head. Although he had a strong build, he was believed to have been in poor health. The man had worn dentures, as well as a fake gold ring.

It was believed that the man may have once been in the military. His arm, which had been fractured, had a type of surgical pin that was often used in military field hospitals.

Testing couldn't determine the date of the man's death. However, the carpet that he had been covered by dated back to the 1970s.

In August of 2015, it was thought that there was a new lead in the case when authorities learned that a man named Gustav Prilepok had been murdered in West Bloomfield Township back in 1991. Prilepok had been murdered by his wife, Janea, and her son, Jan Borek. Gustav Prilepok had a military background.

Janea Prilepok and Jan Borek allegedly hid Gustav's body in a roll of carpet or linoleum before reporting him missing. The duo later confessed to Prilepok's murder, but his body was never found.

There were some discrepancies in the two cases that didn't add up and left Plymouth Township police skeptical, however. Prilepok didn't wear dentures, like the body that was found. It was also thought that Prilepok had a large waist.

Janea and Borek were later deported before they ever disclosed the location of Prilepok's whereabouts.

So, who was the Plymouth County "John Doe"? The world may never know!

Michigan's Most Haunted Lighthouses

There are more than 120 lighthouses in Michigan, so it may come as no surprise to learn that some of them are rumored to be haunted.

According to *Coastal Living* magazine, the following lighthouses are some of the most haunted lighthouses in the entire country:

- Seul Choix Lighthouse – The lighthouse is believed to be haunted by former keeper Captain Joseph Townsend, who died in the keeper's house one winter during the early 1900s. His body couldn't be buried for months due to the winter weather conditions, so his corpse was stored in the basement. It's for that reason that people believe Townsend haunts the lighthouse, which is located in Gulliver, Michigan. People have reported smelling cigars. Museum staff members have also reported unexplained changes in the kitchen's chairs and place settings. There have even been claims of sightings of a ghostly male apparition looking through the windows.

- Big Bay Point Lighthouse – Located on the Michigan Upper Peninsula, Big Bay Point Lighthouse was once thought to be haunted by lighthouse keeper William Prior. Prior became the lighthouse's keep back in 1896. Today, the lighthouse is now a bed and breakfast. Prior was allegedly still haunting the place until an angry innkeeper by the name of Linda Gamble told him off after he slammed the kitchen cabinet doors, causing her to wake up. Since then, no one has heard from William Prior (or the other five ghosts that were thought to haunt the lighthouse, too).

- Old Presque Isle Lighthouse – Although this lighthouse, located on Lake Huron, was only functional for 31 years, it's believed to be incredibly haunted. First, there's the ghost of the screaming woman. She's believed to be the ghost of a lighthouse keeper's wife who was once locked away in the tower. Then there's the ghost of George Parris. Parris and his wife lived in the keeper's cottage during the 1990s. They ran the museum and gave tours of the lighthouse. Every night since Parris died, the lighthouse's light turns on at dusk and turns off at dawn. That in itself might not seem strange if it weren't for the fact that the light had been permanently disabled *and* the Coast Guard has since removed the old light from the tower, but it still continues to shine every night.

- White River Light Station – The Great Lakes lighthouse is thought to be haunted by

Captain William Robinson, the first lighthouse keeper who eventually died in the building. People have reported hearing unexplained pacing sounds upstairs, which are believed to be Robinson tending to his lighthouse. It's also been said that when the museum curator leaves a dust rag near one of the display cases, the rag is always removed and the case has been dusted. It's thought that Robinson's wife, Sarah, is responsible for the ghostly dustings.

The Murder of David Widlak

The murder of David Widlak is one of Oakland County, Michigan's creepiest unsolved mysteries.

One morning in September of 2010, Community Central Bank's CEO, David Widlak, was missing. His car was empty in the parking lot and he couldn't be found in the building. The maintenance worker who discovered the empty car later visited his office, which he found to be a complete mess, before calling the authorities.

No one had seen David Widlak since he had left his office the night before. Surveillance cameras showed Widlak leaving the building around eight o'clock p.m. He waited at the door for a total of 26 seconds before walking out of the building by himself.

While it was thought that Widlak may have chosen to

leave, the authorities still declared him a missing person.

A few weeks passed, and Widlak didn't show up. Authorities suspected that Widlak may have been the victim of foul play. Several weeks before his disappearance, David Widlak had purchased a semiautomatic handgun.

It's unknown if he bought it for self-defense or if he planned to commit suicide. What *is* known is that Widlak *and* his gun both went missing from his office that day, even though he typically left it in his office overnight.

About a month after he went missing, David Widlak's decomposed body was discovered floating in a lake, which was located just four miles away from the bank.

During the autopsy, the coroner said that there were no signs of injuries on Widlak's body. He concluded that Widlak had killed himself.

Widlak's family weren't convinced, however. They arranged for a second autopsy. Somehow, the first coroner had missed the bullet that was found in Widlak's neck. Widlak had been shot in the back of the head, execution style. His gun was discovered in the same area where his body was found.

Widlak's family accused the first medical examiner of

a cover-up. The coroner argued that he had misread the X-ray results.

David Widlak's murder is considered to be an unsolved homicide, though there is a prominent theory about why he might have been killed.

Prior to his death, Widlak had been seeking new investors. It's believed that his murder might have been linked to a business deal.

It was also suggested that Widlak's death may have had something to do with the bank's debt. The bank allegedly lost $13 million during the first half of the year.

Though some have said that Widlak was a gambling addict, which may have had something to do with his death, those claims were denied by his co-workers and the Sherriff.

That being said, there are some who still believe that Widlak did commit suicide. Dr. Spitz, who performed the first autopsy, felt that it was still possible for the wound to have been self-inflicted, despite its location. Dr. Dragovich, who performed the second autopsy, felt it was near impossible to shoot oneself in the back of the head.

The Disappearance of Jimmy Hoffa

Jimmy Hoffa, who was pardoned by Richard Nixon in 1971, had spent four years in prison for crimes he committed when he was president of the union, which was the largest in America. His crimes included bribery, mail fraud, and jury-tampering.

Hoffa went missing in Michigan in 1975, never to be seen again.

He was last seen at the parking lot of Red Fox restaurant in Bloomfield Township in July of 1975.

Hoffa had told people he was going to the restaurant to meet Mafia leaders Anthony Giacalone and Anthony Provenzano. Hoffa and Provenzano had previously been close, as Provenzano was also a Teamster in New Jersey.

At the time of their meeting, however, the two were enemies. During the two years leading up to his disappearance, Hoffa had asked Provenzano for help in supporting him to get back into office. Provenzano didn't want to listen to him and even made threats about killing him and kidnapping his granddaughters. Provenzano's threats weren't taken lightly due to his mafia involvement. At least two of Provenzano's opponents were believed to have been murdered and many had been physically assaulted.

Detroit mafia Kingpin Anthony Giacalone and his brother Vito had visited Hoffa's Lake Orion on multiple occasions to set up a "peace meeting" between Hoffa and Provenzano.

Hoffa's son was worried about him. He believed that Giacalone was setting his father up for a hit. Even Hoffa was allegedly nervous every time Giacalone visited him.

Hoffa's friend from prison, Louis Linteau, was known to be his off-the-record "secretary." If anyone needed to meet with Hoffa, they had to go through Linteau first. Linteau had arranged a dinner meeting between Hoffa and the Giacalone brothers on July 26th. During that dinner, they informed him that he was to meet Provenzano on July 30th.

On July 30th, Hoffa stopped by Linteau's house. Linteau wasn't home, so Hoffa went to his office. Since Linteau was out to lunch, Hoffa left a message.

At 2:15 p.m., Hoffa called his wife from a pay phone, complaining that Tony Giacalone hadn't shown up. He believed he was stood up. Hoffa told his wife he would be home around 4 p.m.

Hoffa was seen pacing the Red Fox's parking lot. Two men allegedly saw Hoffa come out of the Red Fox after having lunch and stopped by to shake his hand.

At 3:27 p.m., Linteau received a phone call from Hoffa. Hoffa complained the Giacalone was late. Linteau told Hoffa to calm down and come by his office on the way home, to which Hoffa agreed.

Jimmy Hoffa never went home that night.

Hoffa's wife called their son and daughter at 7 a.m. the next morning to let them know that Jimmy had never come home the night before.

Hoffa's daughter said she had a "vision" of her father. She claimed that in her vision, her father was slumped over and dead, wearing a dark polo t-shirt.

That morning, Louis Linteau went to the restaurant parking lot, where he found Hoffa's car. The car had been left unlocked, but there was no sign of Hoffa or any clues of what may have happened to him. Linteau called the police. That evening, Hoffa's son filed a missing person report.

Multiple law enforcement agencies, including the FBI, became involved in the investigation. After years of investigating, the case remains unsolved.

Provenzano and Giacalone both denied that they had planned to meet Hoffa at the restaurant that day. They also weren't believed to be near the restaurant that day.

Jimmy Hoffa's body was never found, but he was declared legally dead in 1982—two years after Hoffa's wife had died. Her children believed that she had died of a broken heart.

In 1989, Kenneth Walton, who was then head of the FBI office in Detroit and part of the investigation, claimed that he knew what had happened to Hoffa. Walton said it would never be prosecuted, however, because it would mean divulging informants.

In 2001, DNA testing confirmed that Hoffa's hair had been found in the car of his friend Chuckie O'Brien on July 30th, 1975. It had been long thought that O'Brien may have played a role in Hoffa's disappearance. O'Brien denied these claims.

Author Charles Brant claimed in his book, *I heard You Paint Houses: Frank "The Irishman" Sheeran and the Closing of the Case on Jimmy Hoffa*, that mob killer Frank Sheeran had confessed to killing Hoffa. Sheeran allegedly claimed to shoot Hoffa twice behind the right ear and that Hoffa's body was later cremated. Sheeran also allegedly made his confession to reporters. However, a DNA test of blood that was discovered in the Detroit house where Sheeran said the murder took place did not match Hoffa's.

Author Richard Kuklinski had another slightly more chilling theory. He claimed in his book, *The Iceman: Confessions of a Mafia Contract Killer*, that Hoffa's body had been placed in a 50-gallon drum and set on fire for 30 minutes or so before the drum was welded shut and buried in a junkyard. Kuklinski claimed that the drum was later dug up and sold as scrap metal, along with hundreds of cars, to Japan, in which it was to be used to make new cars.

Brothers Thomas and Stephen Andretta were named as suspects in the investigation. The brothers were New Jersey Teamsters associated with the Genovese crime family. Thomas Andretta was also said to be trusted by Anthony Provenzano.

Thomas Andretta died in 2019 after serving time in prison for racketeering.

To this day, no one knows for sure what happened to Jimmy Hoffa.

RANDOM FACTS

1. The Oakland County Child Killer was believed to have been responsible for the homicides of at least two girls and two boys in Oakland County, Michigan between 1976 and 1977. Several suspects were believed to be the culprit, including serial killer John Wayne Gacy. It's unknown, to this day, who the killer was.

2. The Higgins Lake Monster was first thought to be lurking in the waters of Higgins Lake in Roscommon County in 2006. The creature has been described as yellow and slimy with bony spikes on its reptile-like spine. The Higgins Lake Monster allegedly attacked a woman's canoe, causing her to have to swim to shore. Back in 2012, a 43.5" northern pike was found in Higgins Lake, which was suspected of being the monster. However, there have been reported sightings since then, meaning the Higgins Lake Monster is still lurking in the lake's waters.

3. A 16-year-old boy named Erik Cross was killed in 1983 after going to a party in his hometown of Vicksburg, Michigan. Cross was struck and killed by a car and left to die in the road. Locals call the road where it happened "Blood Run."

4. The Whitney Restaurant, which is located on Woodward Avenue in Detroit, is thought to be haunted. It was the former mansion of David Whitney, Jr., one of the richest lumber barons in the Midwest. Built in 1894, the mansion was made up of 21,000 square feet. The mansion was restored during the 1980s and since then, there have been reports of what is believed to be paranormal activity. People have seen unexplained shadow-like apparitions on the second floor and heard unusual voices. People also claim to get strange feelings that they attribute to ghosts. Paranormal investigators have also done recordings at the Whitney and heard disembodied voices actually *answering* them, as well as piano music. David Whitney and his wife both passed away in the mansion. It's believed that their ghosts have never left!

5. Fort Mackinac is thought to be one of the most haunted places in all of Michigan. There have been reports of apparitions of soldiers walking the Rifle Range Trail, as well as apparitions of limbs at the hospital. Furniture has also been said to move on its own. People have reported hearing children crying at the fort, which makes sense; at least 13 children died at the fort due to typhoid fever, tuberculosis, and other diseases. It's thought that the children's cries are the lost

souls of these children. There have also been reports of a phantom fife player near the Fort's North Sally Port Entrance during the early hours of the morning.

6. There's a place known as "The Drowning Pool" on Mackinac Island. It's located between the downtown area and the Mission Point Resort. The Drowning Pool is a 20-foot drop-off in a lagoon that has a haunting past. During the late 1700s and early 1800s, there were brothels on the island. Seven women were accused of witchcraft and seducing soldiers, married men, and fur traders to come to their houses. According to the legend, rocks were tied around the women's ankles and they were thrown into the lagoon. Those who sank were believed to be innocent. Todd Clemens, a paranormal researcher in the area, believes that the Drowning Pool is haunted by the spirits of the accused women. Unexplained shadows and loud splashing noises have been reported at the Drowning Pool.

7. The Nain Rouge is one of Michigan's biggest urban legends. "Nain Rouge" is French for "red dwarf." According to local lore, Detroit's founder Antoine de la Mothe Cadillac came across a demon-like creature that called itself the Nain Rouge. It was believed that the Nain Rouge cursed the city of Detroit. Reports of the creature

have emerged over the years, generally during the city's most tragic events. There were alleged sightings of the monster back in 1805 when a fire took place, which almost burnt Detroit to the ground. There was also reports of the Nain Rouge during the 1968 riots. During a snowstorm in 1976, authorities saw what they believed to be a child climbing a utility pole, but it turned out to be the Nain Rouge. Today, the Nain Rouge has become an important part of the city's history and culture, with Detroit residents embracing it. There's an annual parade that celebrates the monster.

8. Legend says that the Michigan Bell Telephone Company was built where the Judd-White House used to be. Located in downtown Grand Rapids, the house had a haunting past. In the early 1900s, a happy couple named Warren and Virginia Randall moved into the Judd-White House. Warren worked on the Indiana Railroad and had a work accident that caused him to lose a leg. Warren became paranoid and suspected that Virginia was having an affair, causing their marriage to suffer. Virginia left him, but Warren convinced her to come back to the house to see him. After he had lured her into the house, Warren bludgeoned Virginia with his wooden leg. Then he tore a gas fixture from the wall. As

the fumes filled the air, Warren slit his own throat with a razor. Police discovered the couple's bodies after there were reports of a horrible odor. The house was eventually torn down. The Michigan Bell Telephone Company built its offices on the vacant lot. People have reportedly heard the couples screaming at night and a tapping sound that's believed to be Warren's wooden leg.

9. The historic Calumet Theater, which is located in Calumet, MI in the Upper Peninsula, is thought to be haunted. The theater is believed to be haunted by the ghost of Madame Helen Modjeska, a Polish opera singer who performed at the theater prior to her death in 1909. Theater actors and guests have claimed to see Madame Modjeska since her death. In 1958, an actress had a hard time remembering her lines. She claimed to see Modjeska mouthing the lines to her on the theater balcony. In addition to reports of Madame Modjeska's ghostly apparition, people have also claimed to experience unexplained cold breezes, doors locking, and music.

10. The Paulding Light is an unexplained light that can be found in a valley near Paulding, Michigan. First recognized during the 1960s, the light has been described as a single, bright light. Although Michigan Tech students have said that they could

recreate the Paulding Light if a car was driven along US 45 at a certain spot with its headlights on, people still often attribute the light to ghosts. In the most popular tale, a railroad worker was killed in a train crash. The worker used a lantern to notify cars that the train was coming. Some believe that the Paulding Light is the railroad worker, still using his lantern to try to warn people.

11. It has been said that you can come face-to-face with the Ada Witch in a cemetery in Ada, Michigan. According to the local lore, a man who lived during the 1800s learned that his wife was having an affair. When he caught them in the act, the man murdered his wife before fighting her lover in a battle that caused *both* of them to die. The woman is known, today, as the Ada Witch. She is allegedly buried under a broken tombstone in Findley Cemetery. People have claimed to hear the sound of two men fighting, sometimes followed by the apparition of the Ada Witch. Ada is known to wear white and is often found near her own grave—even though evidence has suggested that the grave in question is actually that of a woman who died of typhoid, rather than the adulterous woman.

12. The Holly Hotel, which is located in Holly, MI, has managed to survive two fires. Both fires took

place on January 19th; one of the fires was in 1931 and the other was in 1996, exactly 65 years apart from one another. Some believe that supernatural forces are to blame. The hotel is said to be haunted. Guests have claimed to smell cigar smoke, which is thought to be due to the original owner of the hotel, who loved cigars. Then there's the perfume scent, which is attributed to the ghost of Nora Kane. Kane was known to wear a lot of perfume and loved music when she was alive. People have claimed to hear her humming or singing. The spirit of a little girl is also believed to haunt the Holly Hotel's kitchen. On the bright side, all of the ghosts that haunt the hotel are believed to be friendly!

13. The Snake Goddess of Belle Isle is one of the most popular legends in the Detroit area. The legend goes like this: an Ottawa Chief who was called Sleeping Bear wished to protect his beautiful daughter from her many suitors, so he threw a blanket over her canoe and sent her up the Detroit River. The wind, which was also said to be taken by her beauty, was so strong that it blew her blanket away and caused her canoe to go downriver. Although the girl was kidnapped on her voyage, the wind was able to intervene and rescued her. The wind then sent her back home to Sleeping Bear, who then proceeded to

put his daughter on Belle Isle. Sleeping Bear asked the spirits to protect his daughter. The spirits did as he asked by surrounding the island with snakes, giving his daughter the ability to transform into a white deer when she was at risk of being captured, and making her immortal. The girl became known as the Snake Goddess. People who visit Belle Isle often say they see white deer wandering the island.

14. In July of 1960, a woman named Frances Lacey was found dead on Mackinac Island. Her body was discovered under a pile of brush below Stonecliffe Mansion. The cause of death? She had been strangled in her own underwear. Lacey had left her hotel and was on her way to a cabin her family had been staying at the British Landing. She never made it there, however. Her purse was found first, followed by her shoes, and eventually her body. She had been robbed, raped, and murdered. A recently caught serial killer named Hugh Bion Morse was suspected of the murder. However, no evidence was ever found that linked him or anyone else to the crime. To date, the case remains Mackinac Island's biggest unsolved mystery.

15. If you travel on Strasburg Road in the Detroit/Grosse Isle area after the sun has set, you might encounter a young girl. When you stop at

a red light, the girl may approach your car and knock on the window. Be careful, though. She's said to be searching for the driver who killed her during the early 1940s. The killer allegedly hasn't been found.

16. South Manitou Island is the most haunted place in Michigan, according to *Thrillist*. The island is located 16 miles off the coast of Leelanau Peninsula. With its deserted shoreline, 300-foot sand dunes, and empty campgrounds, the island is known to have an eerie, ghost town feeling to it. According to legends, a ship with passengers who had died from cholera once stopped at the island. Sailors allegedly buried the victims in a big grave. It's been said that some of the passengers were still alive at the time they were buried. There are also two cemeteries on the island, as well as a cedar forest where ghostly voices have been reported. There's also the shipwreck of the *SS* Francisco Morazan, which crashed on the island's shore in the 1960s. A young boy allegedly died on the shipwreck when he tried to explore it on his own.

17. The Doherty Hotel in Clare, Michigan is said to be one of the most haunted spots in the state. The hotel has been owned by the Doherty family since it first opened in the 1920s. During the prohibition, the Doherty Hotel was a speakeasy.

In addition to providing illegal alcohol, there was also backroom gambling and adult entertainment. The Mafia and Purple Gang also hung out there. Back in 1938, one of the most famous murders in all of Michigan happened at the hotel. Isaiah Leebove, who was formerly of the Purple Gang, was shot to death by his cousin in the hotel's bar. It's believed that Isaiah Leebove's ghost haunts the hotel, along with Helen Doherty. It has been said that Helen Doherty's voice can be heard in a back room, which is where her body had been placed after she died.

18. During an episode of *Ghost Hunters*, Amy Bruni said that she believes Mackinac Island may be so haunted because of how the island hasn't changed much over the years. The island doesn't allow vehicles and has its old-style charms. But it's almost as though the island is stuck in time—leaving the spirits to be stuck there with it.

19. The Torch Lake Monster is a bit of myth turned real… *maybe*. Dave Foley, who was a counselor at Camp Hayo-Went-Ha during the 1960s and 1970s, says he started the myth of the Torch Lake Monster to entertain campers. However, there's a legend of an actual lake monster, which is thought to be a "sea panther." The monster allegedly has the head of a cat and the body of a lizard.

20. There's a legend about the beach at Bete Grise on the southern Keweenaw Peninsula. The tale goes like this: A Native American woman's lover was taken by Lake Superior. The woman lived the rest of her life crying out for him. It's been said that the sand still calls his name today, but *only* if you pat or brush the sand with your hand. This allegedly only works if you're on the beach. If you remove the sand, you won't be able to hear the woman's voice.

Test Yourself – Questions

1. Michigan's most famous lake monster is named:

   a. Pressie
   b. Nessie
   c. Bessie

2. The Nain Rouge is said to haunt which of Michigan's cities?

   a. Lansing
   b. Detroit
   c. Ann Arbor

3. Mackinac Island's "Drowning Pool" is thought to be haunted due to its history of:

   a. Witch killings
   b. Native American spirits
   c. The murder of Harvey

4. Belle Isle is thought to be haunted by:

   a. The Melon Heads
   b. The Michigan Dogman
   c. The Snake Goddess

5. Which of Michigan's lighthouses is thought to be haunted by the ghost of William Prior?

   a. Seoul Choix Lighthouse
   b. Old Presque Isle Lighthouse
   c. Big Bay Point Lighthouse

Answers

1. a.
2. b.
3. a.
4. c.
5. c.

OTHER BOOKS IN THIS SERIES

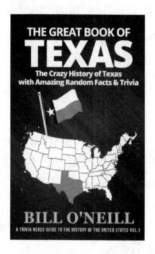

Are you looking to learn more about Texas? Sure, you've heard about the Alamo and JFK's assassination in history class, but there's so much about the Lone Star State that even natives don't know about. In this trivia book, you'll journey through Texas's history, pop culture, sports, folklore, and so much more!

In The Great Book of Texas, some of the things you will learn include:

Which Texas hero isn't even from Texas?

Why is Texas called the Lone Star State?

Which hotel in Austin is one of the most haunted hotels in the United States?

Where was Bonnie and Clyde's hideout located?

Which Tejano musician is buried in Corpus Christi?

What unsolved mysteries happened in the state?

Which Texas-born celebrity was voted "Most Handsome" in high school?

Which popular TV show star just opened a brewery in Austin?

You'll find out the answers to these questions and many other facts. Some of them will be fun, some of them will creepy, and some of them will be sad, but all of them will be fascinating! This book is jampacked with everything you could have ever wondered about Texas.

Whether you consider yourself a Texas pro or you know absolutely nothing about the state, you'll learn something new as you discover more about the state's past, present, and future. Find out about things that weren't mentioned in your history book. In fact, you might even be able to impress your history teacher with your newfound knowledge once you've finished reading! So, what are you waiting for? Dive in now to learn all there is to know about the Lone Star State!

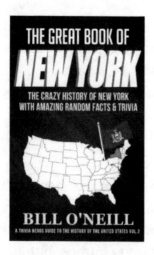

Want to learn more about New York? Sure, you've heard about the Statue of Liberty, but how much do you really know about the Empire State? Do you know why it's even called the Empire State? There's so much about New York that even state natives don't know. In this trivia book, you'll learn more about New York's history, pop culture, folklore, sports, and so much more!

In The Great Book of New York, you'll learn the answers to the following questions:

- Why is New York City called the Big Apple?
- What genre of music started out in New York City?
- Which late actress's life is celebrated at a festival held in her hometown every year?
- Which monster might be living in a lake in New York?

171

- Was there really a Staten Island bogeyman?
- Which movie is loosely based on New York in the 1800s?
- Which cult favorite cake recipe got its start in New York?
- Why do the New York Yankees have pinstripe uniforms?

These are just a few of the many facts you'll find in this book. Some of them will be fun, some of them will be sad, and some of them will be so chilling they'll give you goosebumps, but all of them will be fascinating! This book is full of everything you've ever wondered about New York.

It doesn't matter if you consider yourself a New York state expert or if you know nothing about the Empire State. You're bound to learn something new as you journey through each chapter. You'll be able to impress your friends on your next trivia night!

So, what are you waiting for? Dive in now so you can learn all there is to know about New York!

THE GREAT BOOK OF
CALIFORNIA
THE CRAZY HISTORY OF CALIFORNIA
WITH AMAZING RANDOM FACTS & TRIVIA

BILL O'NEILL
A TRIVIA NERDS GUIDE TO THE HISTORY OF THE UNITED STATES VOL. 3

Are you interested in learning more about California? Sure, you've heard of Hollywood, but how much do you really know about the Golden State? Do you know how it got its nickname or what it was nicknamed first? There's so much to know about California that even people born in the state don't know it all. In this trivia book, you'll learn more about California's history, pop culture, folklore, sports, and so much more!

In The Great Book of California, you'll discover the answers to the following questions

- Why is California called the Golden State?
- What music genres started out in California?
- Which celebrity sex icon's death remains a mystery?
- Which serial killer once murdered in the state?
- Which childhood toy started out in California?

- Which famous fast-food chain opened its first location in the Golden State?
- Which famous athletes are from California?

These are just a few of the many facts you'll find in this book. Some of them will be entertaining, some of them will be tragic, and some of them may haunt you, but all of them will be interesting! This book is full of everything you've ever wondered about California and then some!

Whether you consider yourself a California state expert or you know nothing about the Golden State, you're bound to learn something new in each chapter. You'll be able to impress your college history professor or your friends during your next trivia night!

What are you waiting for? Get started to learn all there is to know about California!

MORE BOOKS BY BILL O'NEILL

I hope you enjoyed this book and
learned something new. Please feel free
to check out some of my previous
books on Amazon.

**IF YOU LIKED THIS BOOK, I
WOULD REALLY APPRECIATE
IF YOU COULD LEAVE A SHORT
REVIEW ON AMAZON.**

Printed in the USA
CPSIA information can be obtained
at www.ICGtesting.com
LVHW011800180524
780707LV00001B/239